Manet

Phidal

“In the studio, fury was released onto the empty canvas, with such confusion that it seemed as if he had never painted before.”

Stéphane Mallarmé

“Who is it who throws stones at Impressionism? It’s Manet.
Who is it who cries out furiously against charlatanism? It’s Manet.
But... who is it who is dividing everyone up into factions?
Everyone in Paris knows, that’s Manet too. It’s all Manet.”

These ironic verses, written in 1877 by a critic who was also something of a poet, were meant to sum up the personality of the painter Edouard Manet.

Who was this contradictory character, Manet? Born into a bourgeois family who provided him with everything he needed, he was a man who rebelled against the conventions of his class, yet nevertheless remained an integral part of it. He was a man who challenged society in spite of himself, as he pursued and proclaimed freedom of expression, yet, nevertheless, sought official recognition of his talent and yearned to be accepted in respectable drawing rooms. On the surface, he was a conformist who refused to be seen as working outside the rules of society. Yet his paintings provoked constant scandal.

What was Manet seeking? While wanting to maintain a respect for tradition he breathed new life into painting, trying to get to the essence of art by freeing it from all intellectual concerns, creating new paintings where ideas and subjects were only pretexts for other things. As he pursued this, he managed to turn upside down the dominant forces of the day, characterised by a lack of individuality and rigid conformity (one painting could only be distinguished from another by its subject matter). He sought success and public recognition yet created works that were a constant challenge to a public to whom he was unwilling to make any concessions.

How did his contemporaries look upon him? To traditionalists, who would never accept a painting composed so daringly of brushstrokes and colours with no transition, he was a revolutionary. Painters of the next generation, however, who chastised him for his attachment to the Salon and the old masters, accused him of being a traditionalist. “He doesn’t paint a single stroke without thinking of the masters,” said the young Degas of him. These constant contradictions that marked the life of the man and the career of the artist, were witness to the constant sincerity of a painter who refused to compromise. Far from representing sterile contradictions, they point to an extraordinary synthesis of past and present. By the end of his life, Manet enjoyed unequalled success and was acclaimed by the public and his peers alike.

Thus, in the end, he prevailed; his march against the tide succeeded in every sense, from the Salon to the avant-garde, from the present to the future.

Edouard Manet was born in Paris on the 23rd of January 1832 into a comfortable bourgeois family. His father Auguste was a well-placed government official in the Ministry of the Interior and his mother Eugénie Désirée Fournier was the refined and well-educated daughter of a diplomat. Edouard had two brothers, Eugène, a year younger than he, who married Berthe Morisot, and Gustave. At the age of twelve, he enrolled in the College Rollin where he met Antonin Proust, another young student who would become a friend for life and with whom he studied drawing. In those days Edouard often went to the Louvre on Sundays with his maternal uncle, who encouraged his budding artistic talent.

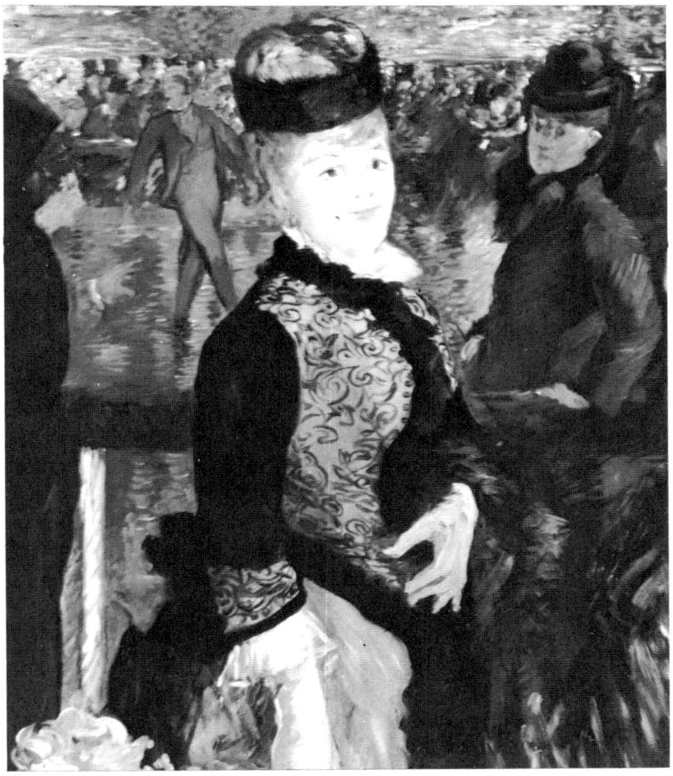

Skating (detail) - 1877. The Fogg Art Museum, Harvard University, Cambridge, Mass. - Bequest of M. Maurice Wertheim

Manet’s artistic vocation, however, was to be impeded by his father who presented him with a choice of two professions: he could either become a lawyer or a naval officer. Although he failed the entrance exam for the Naval School, Manet set off on a cargo ship bound for Rio de Janeiro as a student pilot and spent several months on board. Back in France with notebooks full of sketches from his voyage, Manet decided not to enter the competition for a place at the Naval School but instead, to pursue his true vocation. Faced with such resistance, his father finally capitulated and in January 1850 Edouard Manet entered the studios of Thomas Couture as an apprentice. Couture was a fashionable academic painter of the time and Manet spent the next six years studying with him. They turned out to be six years full of conflict between pupil and teacher and constant insubordination on Manet’s part.

During this period, Manet took piano lessons from a young Dutch woman, Suzanne Leenhoff and she ended up pregnant. However, the child born to them, Léon-Edouard, was never officially recognised by Manet as Manet's father was strongly opposed to their union. Indeed, it was not until 1862 after the death of Manet's father, that the two were actually married.

The style of Couture's painting was completely different from Manet's. Besides the rather flat conventional imagery that Couture used, it was their different way of looking at colour that separated the two artists. "You refuse to see the succession of intermediate tones that lead from shadow to light," said Couture to his student. But Manet asserted that it was preferable to go directly from light to shade, because the accumulation of intermediate nuances weakened the vigour of the light and smudged the colours of the shadows that he wanted to emphasise. Ten years before Monet, Manet had invented the idea of pure colour that was to become the basis of Impressionism.

At Easter 1856, Manet left Couture's studio, where everything "before his eyes was useless, the light was false, the shadows false" and the studio seemed like "a tomb." He began travelling, first to Italy, then to The Hague, to Vienna, and to Munich which delighted him. Most often though, he went to the Louvre, excursions which interested him greatly and which were to influence his work. There he copied paintings by Titian, Tintoretto, and Velasquez, and he studied more contemporary painters such as Goya, Daumier, Delacroix, and Courbet. At the Louvre he met other young painters, including Whistler and Fantin-Latour, who also refused all doctrinaire constraints and believed that academic studies were no longer effective.

Manet considered Delacroix his true master and asked him for permission to copy his *Dante and Virgil*. Later, when Manet's first canvas revealing his own style, *The Absinthe Drinker*, was refused by the Salon of 1858, the only voice raised in defence of this masterpiece was Delacroix's. Even Couture voted against his former pupil.

At that time the Salon was the only means by which an artist could become known to the public and mentioned by the press, and thus join the art establishment.

The jury of the Salon, however, was not yet ready to accept Manet's art. Upset by the diversity of artistic currents, it was not prepared for revolutionary change (artists like Courbet, for example, wanted to "translate morals, ideas, and the tone" of his era and make "living art"). The jury was composed of conservative academicians, like Ingres and Couture who, refusing any change, held fast to classic ideals with no curiosity or interest in new ideas and no respect for those who pursued such possibilities.

Finally, however, fate smiled upon Manet and two of his works were accepted by the Salon of 1861. One was *Portrait of Mr. and Mrs. Auguste Manet*, an austere portrait of his parents which represented the end of his "Couture period", and the other was *The Spanish Singer*, which captured the attention of everyone. The lively colours, the charm of the subject, and a pose that was so full of life drew warm praise from the critics. Here, among the same old themes and the imitations of other paintings, was one inspired by real life with an exotic and picturesque subject. Indeed, the canvas was so successful that it won an honourable mention. *The Spanish Singer* also attracted the attention of young painters who were interested in the way that Manet had transformed the style of Goya and Velasquez into modern idiom.

Manet's name began to circulate in the artistic and intellectual milieu of the day. Suddenly, everyone wanted to meet him and people poured into his studio on the rue Guyot to watch him work. Meanwhile, cafés, the privileged places of cultural debate, had become the occasion for social gatherings for many artists, and each one, as well as each group of artists, had his favourite. It mattered little whether it was the Andler Keller, where Courbet and his disciples met, the Brasserie des Martyrs or the elegant Café Tortoni chosen by Manet; what was extraordinary was that everywhere people met to discuss and debate ideas, to challenge and demolish theories. While official circles languished in their monotony, in the cafés life was bubbling away and there was great intellectual ferment. It was not by chance that artists were drawn to Paris from all over, seeking to benefit from this stimulating atmosphere — Pissarro from the Antilles, Monet from Le Havre, Cézanne and Zola from Aix-en-Provence. Paris, as the painter Fantin-Latour wrote in a letter to some English friends, represented "free art." "One doesn't sell anything," he wrote, "but there is freedom here and there are people searching, people fighting, people applauding..." In this flourishing social and intellectual climate Manet met painters, journalists, critics, writers and poets like Astruc, Castagnary, Champfleury and Duranty; with some of them, like Degas, Baudelaire, and later Mallarmé, he formed strong friendships.

In 1862 he painted *Concert in the Tuileries*. In it one can recognise portraits of Baudelaire (in profile) and many of Manet's other new friends and personalities of the day, listening to music in the Tuileries gardens. It was perhaps the first great painting to capture a moment from everyday life, and even if Manet did not yet dream of becoming "the painter of modern life", he interpreted and, in his own way, personified the image of a true artist. In an article he wrote for *Figaro*, Baudelaire said of him, "The true painter will be he who can show us the epic side of everyday life, making us understand how great and poetic we are in our neckties and polished boots." The canvas was exhibited at the Galerie Martinet along with thirteen others Manet had painted. Several of them took as subjects a troupe of Spanish dancers who had come to perform in Paris, whose colourful costumes and picturesque dances had stimulated Manet's enthusiasm for Spain. Among them were *Spanish Dancers*, *Gypsies*, and the famous *Lola de Valence*, which while evoking Goya, display an unusual palette for the time, and the use of wide bold brushstrokes. The sketched figures have an immediacy that goes beyond the limits of perspective and space.

The year 1863 was marked by the birth of the "Salon des Refusés", organised under the patronage of Napoleon III, to pacify the many artists whom the Salon had refused to exhibit, and also to allow the public to form their own judgements about these works. It was the ideal occasion to gather under one roof all those painters who, like Manet, had little to do with the artistic establishment. Manet showed three oil paintings and three etchings there and other artists such as Pissarro, Whistler, Fantin-Latour, and Cézanne also presented their works. When it opened, crowds of spectators poured into the exhibition attracted more by the paintings refused by the Salon than by the boring paintings accepted by it.

For the first time, Manet's work created a scandal – but not for his *Young Man in Spanish Costume*, a portrait of his brother, nor for *Victorine Meurent in Bullfighter's Outfit*, a portrait of his favourite model which shows the persistance of his taste for a colourful palette and for Spain. It was for his large canvas *Luncheon on the Grass* which was declared indecent by the Emperor himself. This tableau, inspired by *The Concert* by Giorgione, shows two elegant young men in modern dress relaxing along the banks of a river with their two nude companions, one next to the water and the other sitting with them. It had not been Manet's intention to stir up controversy; he had simply been searching for a harmony of colours. Nevertheless, the simple scene shocked a puritanical public troubled by what they felt was a vulgar subject. In fact, except for some praise for Pissarro, none of the artists exhibiting enjoyed any real success and the Salon turned out to be truly a salon of rejected paintings, causing Astruc to declare: "One must be twice as strong to stand up against the flood of fools who have stormed in here by the thousands and jeered at everything to excess." Victorine Meurent, Manet's favourite model, continued to appear in his work until 1875. It is she who is portrayed in *Olympia*, the painting which, when it was displayed in the Salon of 1865, caused fresh scandal. This time it took two guards to protect the painting from the blows of umbrellas and walking sticks. Except for a red flower in her hair, a black ribbon around her neck, and a single slipper dangling from her foot, she is quite naked. Before *Olympia*, portrayals of nudes had been more or less idealised; this realistic nude drew insults from all sides. "The skin tones are dirty," said some. "What kind of odalisque is this with its yellow stomach, an ignoble model picked up God knows where..." Only Baudelaire's genial lucidity was able to weigh the profound sense of these reactions. "These bourgeois imbecils who constantly repeat the words 'immoral', 'immorality', 'morality in art', and other stupidities, make me think of Louise Villedieu, a five franc whore who went with me once to the Louvre where she had never been before. Once there, standing in front of the immortal statues and tableaux, she blushed, covered her face and then, clutching my sleeve, asked me how it was possible to show such indecency in public" (*Mon coeur mis à nu*). It has been said that in *Olympia* Manet copied the *Venus of Urbino* by Titian or Goya's *Maja Desnuda* without actually imitating them, for Manet had the courage to paint his own vision of reality.

Even though he had received an honourable mention in the Salon of 1861, in the Salon of 1865, he was derided and insulted. Thus, Manet became famous, but he was oppressed by a renown that was not particularly welcome. Nevertheless, those who wanted to free themselves from the confines of the art establishment were drawn to him and in spite of himself, he found he had become the head of a new movement. The new aspirants met in his studio or at their meeting place, the Café Guerbois, rue des Batignolles.

That same year, 1865, Manet travelled to Spain, eager to get to know the home of the painters whom he loved so well. His brief visit made a profound impression on him and confirmed his admiration for Velasquez, "the painter of painters." The Spanish period in Manet's evolution was marked by canvases with scenes from bullfights that he painted on his return. Manet had left Paris worn down by the polemics created by the Salon, but on his return, a courageous defence of him and some of the other painters by Emile Zola in *L'Evénement* gave him great comfort. Unfortunately it had cost Zola his job on the newspaper.

Excluded from the Universal Exhibition of 1867, with *The Fifer* and *The Tragic Actor* rejected, Manet did not send any other canvases to the Salon. Instead, following the example of Courbet, he had his own pavillion built in the Place de l'Alma where he exhibited his work, comprising of fifty-three paintings and three etchings. At the last minute, Manet finished a large canvas for the exhibition, *The Execution of Maximilian*, inspired by the tragic events of June 1867. Because of political pressure, however, he was not allowed to show it. Introductory notes for the exhibition, probably written by Astruc, invited viewers not to look at works "without defects" but "sincere works".

Unfortunately the exhibition did not receive the hoped – for success. Once more Zola came to Manet's defence and dedicated an in-depth study to him in *Revue du XIXe siècle*. In return, Manet dedicated a portrait to his writer-friend, which he presented to the Salon of '68 along with *Woman with Parrot*. The *Portrait of Emile Zola* shows the writer in his chambers, sitting at his desk surrounded by books and pamphlets, among which, one can discern the one he wrote about Manet. The critics reproached Manet for making the decor so prominent in relation to both the subject and the expression of his thoughts. *Woman with Parrot*, is another portrait of Victorine Meurent, wearing a pink gown and standing next to a superb parrot on a grey perch. The pictoral elements are reduced to two zones, one in the light where the artist has placed the woman and the other in shadow. As usual, colour and light are Manet's two centres of interest.

At the Louvre, where she was copying paintings and drawings, Manet met Berthe Morisot, a very talented young painter who was to become his sister-in-law and for a time his favourite model. We find her in *The Balcony* wearing a black hat, in *Berthe Morisot with a Bunch of Violets* reclining on a sofa, in *Portrait of Berthe Morisot Reclining* and, her face hidden by a fan, in *Berthe Morisot with Fan*. In *The Balcony*, which with *Lunch in The Studio* was very badly received at the Salon of 1869, one is reminded of *Manolas on the Balcony* by Goya, even though it is a free interpretation. In this canvas Manet eliminated perspective, so that his flat figures seem manipulated like objects in a still-life, empty of any emotional content. All expression of sentiment, so typical of paintings of the past and still part of paintings by Ingres and Delacroix, was banished from these paintings. During this period another woman captured the attention of the painter. Eva Gonzales, a young woman of twenty and the daughter of a well-known writer, became his pupil. Seduced by her beauty, Manet painted her portrait and submitted it to the Salon the next year as *The Music Lesson*, but the portrait was deemed "an abominable flat caricature in oil", painted only to attract attention. Berthe Morisot was very unhappy having a rival in Manet's studio and her correspondence with her sister Edma testifies to this. But she remained a sincere friend of Manet, even apart from their family ties. Certainly Berthe had some part in Manet's conversion to "open air painting" after 1870.

The group of artists who met at the Café Guerbois was united in its intolerance of establishment art, and its willingness to explore new paths; but as each artist had his own vision of art, they limited themselves to painting under the name *The Batignolles Group*. The most important event of the Salon of 1870 was the large canvas entitled *Studio at Batignolles* painted by Fantin-Latour. In the painting, gathered around Manet who is portrayed as the leader of the group sitting at his easel, are Renoir, Astruc, Zola, Maître, Bazille, Monet, and the German painter Schölderer. However, that same year marked the beginning of the Franco-Prussian War and the group dispersed. With the proclamation of the Third Republic, after the disaster of the Sedan and the flight of Napoleon III, Manet, always an ardent republican, joined the National Guard. Monet and Pissarro, meanwhile, found refuge in London. It was not until after the capitulation of Paris that Manet went to rejoin his family in the Midi. When he returned to Paris around the end of the Versailles repression, Manet left his studio (which had been destroyed) in the Rue Guyot and moved to 4, Rue Saint-Petersbourg, a studio that became the subject of several paintings.

While in London, Monet met the art dealer Paul Durand-Ruel who began to buy canvases from artists in the group. He took a great interest in the efforts of these young artists, believing that "a true art dealer should also be a well-informed enthusiast." At the time he was virtually the only one to do so and he became an important moral and economic support to the painters, for except for Manet and Degas who came from wealthy families, they all had serious financial problems. At one time, Manet sold 23 of his paintings for the sum of thirty-five thousand francs. It was by these huge sales that Paul Durand-Ruel linked his career with those of the Batignolles Group.

The next work that Manet exhibited at the Salon of 1873 was a success. Entitled *The Bon Bock*, a portrait of the engraver Bellot sitting at a table at the Café Guerbois, it marked an evolution in

Manet's art. After 1870, influenced by the Naturalist literary movement of which Emile Zola was the foremost representative, the painter worked only in his studio, taking his subjects from popular places and the demi-monde. When Zola published his novel *Nana*, Manet painted a canvas on the same subject with the same title, which was refused by the Salon in 1877. Other paintings from his naturalist period are *Skating*, *The Plum*, *The Laundress* and *Chez le Père Lathuille* which, three years later, Manet presented to the Salon along with his *Portrait of Antonin Proust*.
Meanwhile, tired of having their own work constantly refused by the conservative Salon jury, the members of the Batignolles Group decided to stop submitting them. Manet, whose last works had been favourably received, found himself the only member of the avant-garde at the Salon. Now, in spite of his official victory, the painter began to feel isolated, and accused the other members of the group of giving up too easily, and being responsible, themselves, for their isolation from the Salon. "Why don't you stay with me? You can see that I have connections now," he pleaded in vain. The group wanted to exhibit their works directly to the public by organising a group exhibition.
So, in 1874, in the studio of the photographer Nadar, in the boulevard des Capucines, the first exhibition of the Impressionist painters was held from April 15th to May 15th. (The name came from a painting exhibited by Monet, entitled *Impression: Sunrise*). All of the avant-garde was present: Monet, Renoir, Sisley, Pissarro, Berthe Morisot and Degas. Only Manet was absent. Consistent in his ideas, proud and ambitious, Manet refused to join an initiative he felt was subversive and which would have hindered him in his efforts to become accepted by the establishment. But his attempt to remain aloof was useless. The critics lost no time in establishing a relationship between him and the group in spite of all his efforts to remain separate. Failure hit them all. The exhibition at Nadar's studio did not win public favour and of the three paintings Manet submitted to the Salon, only one was accepted. *The Railway* was given a place of honour, but *The Masked Ball at the Opera* and *The Swallows* were rejected.
Yet, in spite of leading a very different personal life from the others, as an artist, Manet was becoming more and more closely linked to them. His holiday the previous year in Boulogne had already taken him out of the calm atmosphere of his studio and made him appreciate working in the open air. Close to nature and the sea, he found the inspiration for several seascapes such as *The Escape of Rochefort*, *On the Beach at Boulogne* and *The Black Boat at Berck*. He spent the summer of 1874 in Bennevilliers, near Argenteuil, where Monet and Renoir were working. His stimulating meetings with the poet Mallarmé marked the beginning of his use of a lighter palette and Impressionist techniques.
Sudden developments are not usual in an artist's life, however, and Manet had been moving in this direction for a long time. Long years spent with the Impressionists had planted in his mind both the idea of "open air painting" and the interest in light and the changing spectacle of life and nature. Manet had assimilated — perhaps in spite of himself — the ideas of his contemporaries. His own style, once in the vanguard and capable of influencing a whole generation of artists, had become passé. Now it was Manet who was fascinated by the studies of light and optics of Monet and his friends.
That summer, the master often went to visit Monet in Argenteuil, and they worked together painting the Seine with its boats and oarsmen, and mirroring its reflecting colours. It was a happy, serene time for Manet who normally carried with him a hint of melancholy. His paintings are full of bold, exhilarating colour, of inflamed brushstrokes laid side by side without any transition, with violent contrasts of luminous zones so that even the shadows have colour. No longer squirreled away in his studio, Manet was now outside, painting nature as it actually was, as he saw and felt it. Mallarmé shared with him the joy of discovering the open air. The two artists had met daily for years and influenced by each other. One said that "one must paint not the object but the effect that it produced" while the other asserted that poetry should not "name a thing but suggest it."
This genuinely Impressionist experience, lived passionately by Manet, left an ineffable trace in his paintings of the time, with works like *Argenteuil* which he exhibited at the Salon of 1875, *Monet in his Studio Boat*, *The Boat*, and *The Conservatory* as well as his masterpiece of that period *Bar at the Folies-Bergère*. In the last-named work, direct observation of the scene is combined with a splendid invention of composition, namely, a succession of planes achieved through the use of colour.
During this period, Manet suffered an attack of a dreadful disease that would later force him to have his leg amputated and eventually kill him on April 30th, 1882. It was with considerable pain and sacrifice, then, that this work was carried out. But when it was exhibited at the Salon of 1882, it enjoyed great success, winning the official recognition that Manet had so long sought, the Legion of Honour. After the award ceremony, however, Manet said "...it is too late now to make up for 20 years without recognition."
In 1876, Manet began to feel the first pains in his left foot that were to signal the onset of his terrible disease. The same year he reacted to the rejection of *The Artist* by organising an exhibition of his own in his studio and he attracted some 4,000 people. This time the press staunchly supported him. At this exhibition he met Méry Laurent, a woman of the world who became his last great woman friend and his last model. Manet portrayed her in *Woman with Black Hat*, *Méry Laurent with Large Hat* and *Autumn*; it was she who went out to buy the bouquets of roses and lilies for his last paintings when he was too ill to go himself. Manet's studio in rue d'Amsterdam had become a place where all sorts of people came, not only artists but women, friends, and the usual people who frequented artistic circles. Manet often used some of the women as models, painting them nude or half-dressed, wearing simple robes or elegant evening gowns, in oils and pastels, in works like *At the Café*, which portrays women of easy virtue, *Spring*, a portrait of the actress Jeanne Marsy, and *Isabelle Lemonnier*. He also found models at the café-concerts and the Folies-Bergère which he began to visit around 1880 until his illness made it impossible. At the Salon of 1881, the next to last in his lifetime, his works *Pertuiset dressed as a Hunter* and *Portrait of Rochefort* won him a medal. This medal was one he had long desired; it officially made him part of the Salon, and he no longer had to compete or be judged in order to exhibit there.
Alas, it came too late for he died the following year.
If Manet had ever made a reckoning of his life, he would certainly have found it short of the official recognition he so desired, with fame and glory coming too late. To balance that, however, he had enjoyed the friendship and admiration of the liveliest and most brilliant minds of his day. He was also blessed with a fierce tenacity so that he never stopped painting right up until the end. Joys? The satisfaction that comes from having the courage to be oneself, loving life, and knowing how to find "secret voluptuousness in the perfumed refinement of the evening." Disappointments? Perhaps not having been able to see the Hôtel de Ville renovated with frescoes of Paris that he had wanted to paint. And, perhaps knowing that his "scandalous" painting *Olympia* had not been hung in the Louvre as he had hoped (though it eventually was after his death), for he wrote to a critic in 1882, "It would not displease me to read while I am alive the amazing article that you will dedicate to my memory after I am dead."

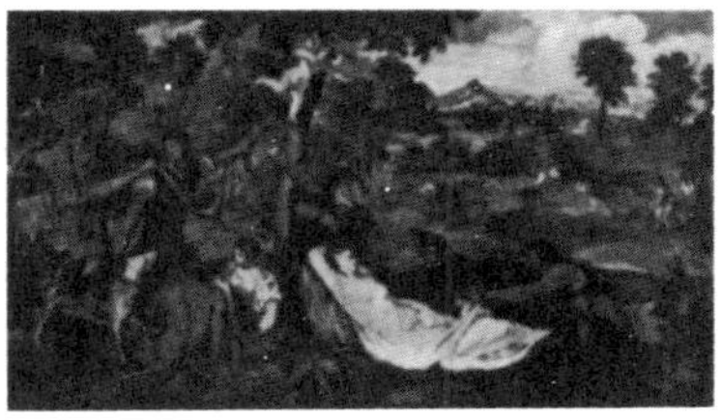

1. Jupiter and Antiope - 1856. Private collection, Paris - *When Manet was just beginning to paint, he often went to the Louvre, fascinated by the masterpieces of the past. Among the many interpretations of paintings he did in those days, is this reproduction of a work by Titian.*

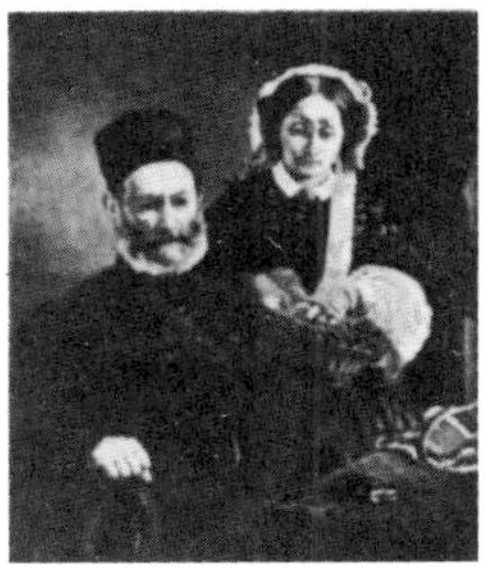

2. Portrait of Mr. and Mrs. Auguste Manet - 1860. Musée d'Orsay, Paris - *This austere portrait, submitted to the Salon of 1861, is the last from the period when Manet was still influenced by Couture, his teacher for six years. Manet's parents are shown here as monuments to bourgeois conservatism. The canvas was deemed vulgar and too realistic — a friend of the family remarked that the couple looked like a pair of concierges.*

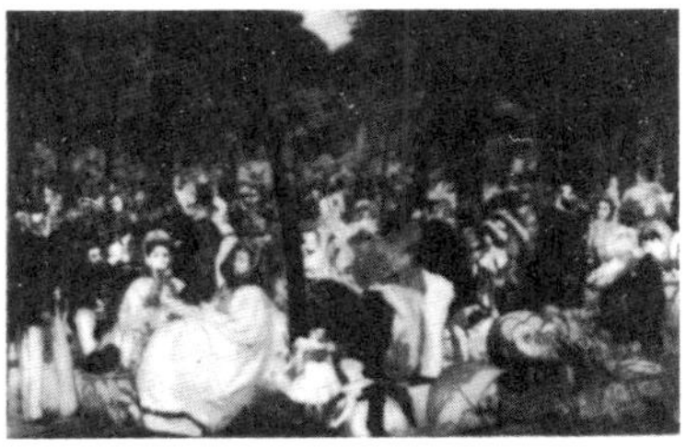

3. Concert in the Tuileries - 1862. National Gallery, London - *This was Manet's first painting using a modern subject. In the crush of people among the trees of the Tuileries Gardens, a favourite haunt for worldly Parisians, one can spot Baudelaire and other artists and personalities of the day.*

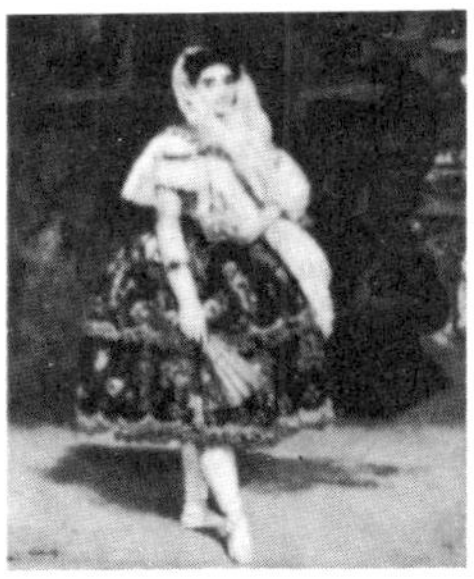

4. Lola de Valence - 1862. Musée du Louvre, Paris - *This realistic portrait of a dancer marked the start of a series of works by Manet inspired by the theatre, a theme that was later much loved and painted by Degas. During his "Spanish" period, Manet painted many such canvases.*

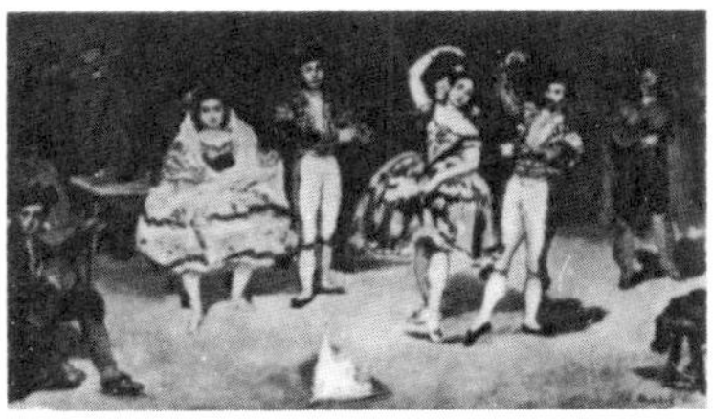

5. Spanish Dancers - 1862. Phillips Collection, Washington, D.C. - *The arrival of a troupe of Spanish dancers in Paris in 1862 was a great source of inspiration for Manet. Although this painting was criticized for its lack of proportion among the different figures, it has a richness of colour that is very pleasing.*

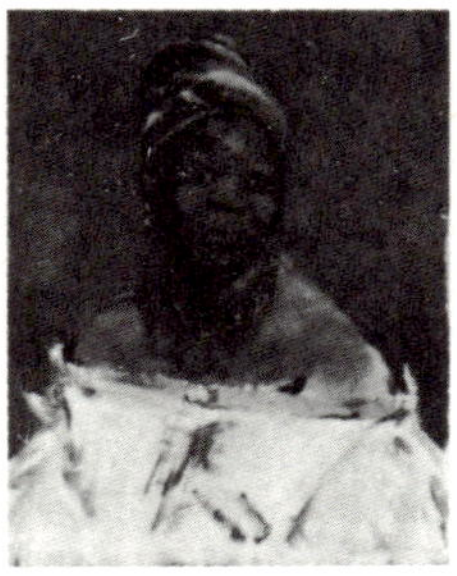

6. The Negress - 1863. Private collection - *This study clearly reveals Manet's new technique which consisted of using short brushstrokes of colour to show alternating light and shade.*

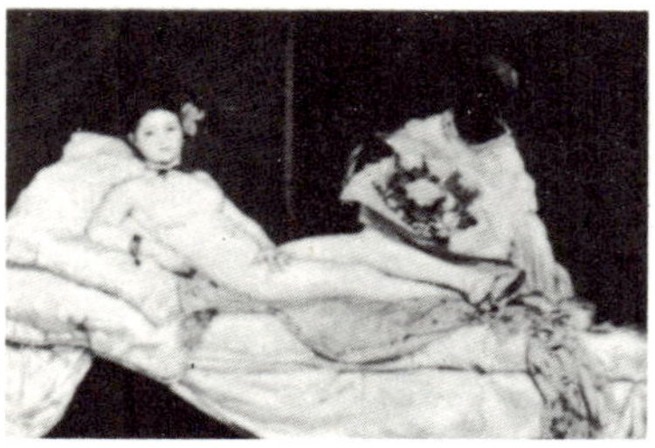

7. Olympia - 1863. Musée d'Orsay, Paris - *This tableau, one of the masterpieces of modern painting, calls to mind another famous work, the "Venus of Urbino" by Titian. Manet's use of flat tints here marks a point of departure in the history of modern art. Its presentation at the Salon of 1865 provoked great scandal.*

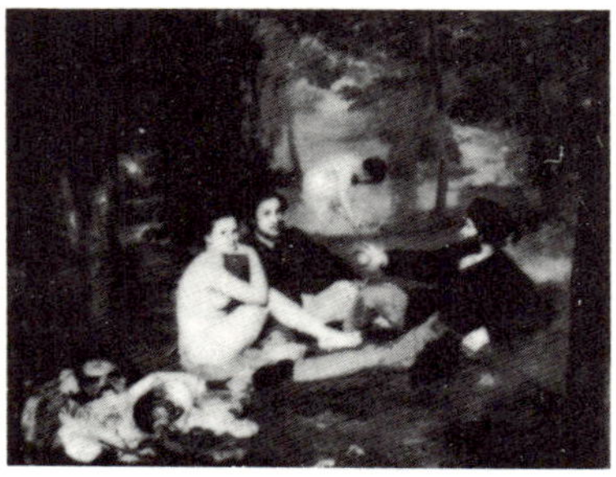

8. Luncheon on the Grass - 1863. Musée d'Orsay, Paris - *In this work, a result of Manet's studies of the nude, the artist was inspired by Giorgione and Raphael. Placed on view at the Salon des Refusés of 1863, it had a profoundly disconcerting effect on the public and was criticized both for its subject matter and the techniques used.*

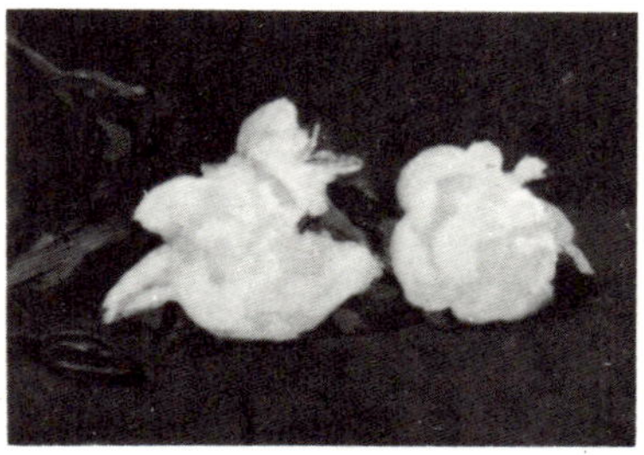

9. Bunch of Peonies and Pruning Scissors - 1864. Musée du Louvre, Paris - *Manet's interest in "pure painting" inevitably led him to the still-life, and there are some astonishing ones painted as part of other compositions (the bouquet of flowers in "Olympia"). However, after 1864 he began to paint them as subjects in their own right.*

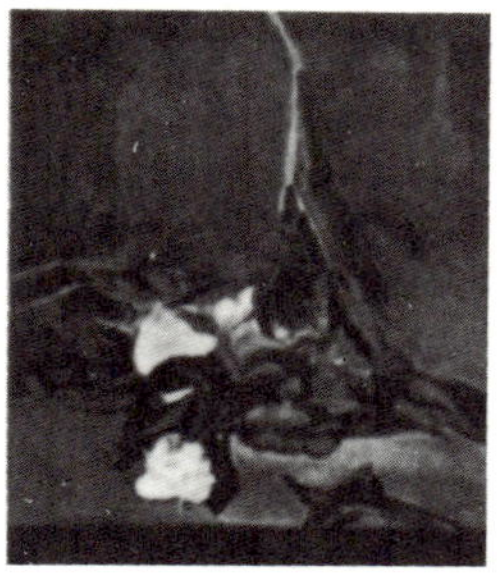

10. Peonies with Scissors - 1864. Musée du Louvre, Paris - *As in his portraits, Manet painted still-lifes realistically, without setting up a situation artificially. The beauty of this painting lies in a bunch of flowers freshly cut.*

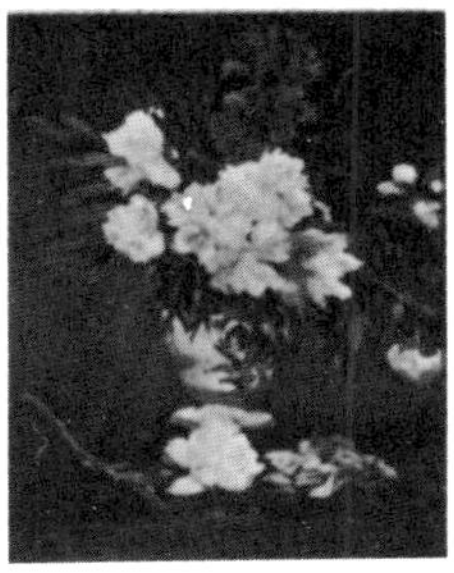

11. Vase of Peonies - 1864. Musée du Louvre, Paris - *Manet loved to paint whatever caught his eye. In this painting, the petals lie fallen on the table just as they probably were when the painter started to paint them.*

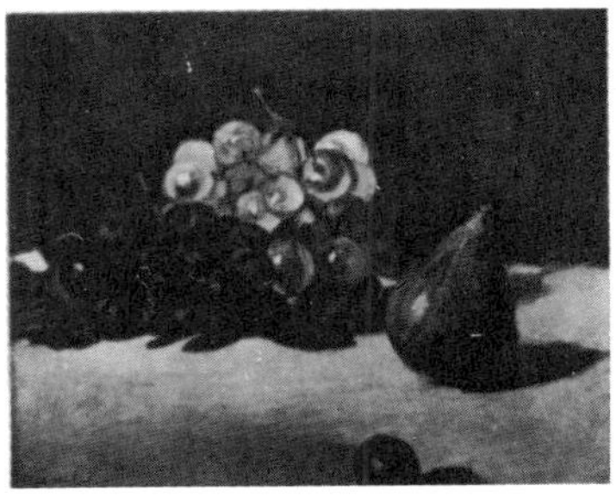

12. Grapes and Figs - 1864. Mrs. Florence Gould Collection, Cannes - *The rich somber tones of this painting bear witness to the strong Spanish influence the painter was under at the time. The light, striking the fruit, creates a brilliant luminosity that invades the entire canvas.*

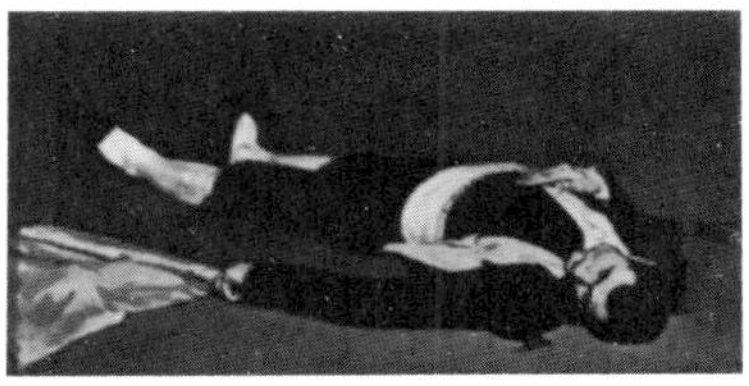

13. The Dead Toreador - 1864. National Gallery of Art, Washington, D.C. - *The tableau "Incident at a Bullfight" had been heavily criticised at the Salon of 1864 because of the cruelty of the scene. So Manet cut the painting into two pieces of which this is the larger.*

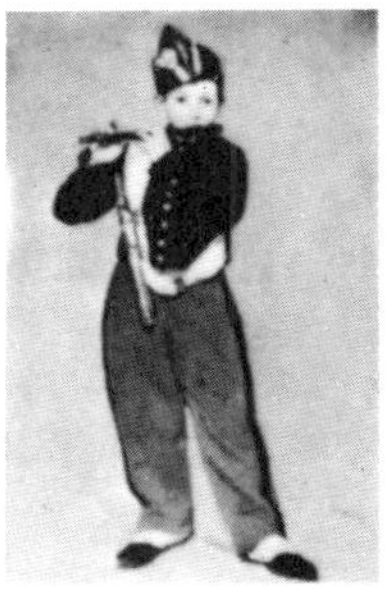

14. The Fifer - 1866. Musée d'Orsay, Paris - *Manet's power of synthesis, the simplification of his drawing, and the contractions of space have been achieved in this painting to the highest degree. There is no background or planes; therefore the young musician, solid and alive, stands out admirably through the use of contrasting colours.*

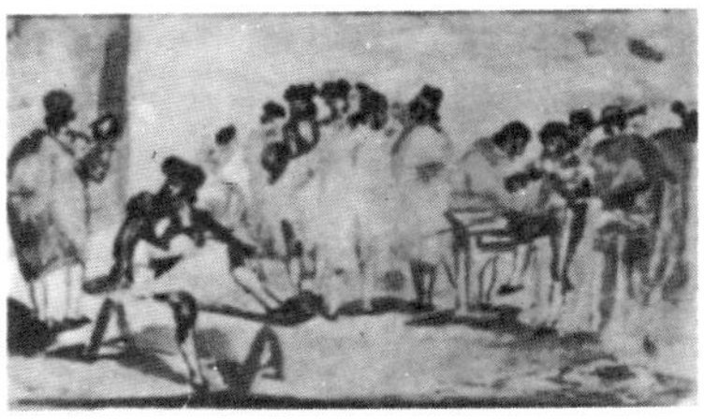

15. The Bullfighters - 1865-66. Hill-Stead Museum, Connecticut - *Manet painted this watercolour following his trip to Spain where he had attended several bullfights. The canvas was left unfinished. Note the strong use of black.*

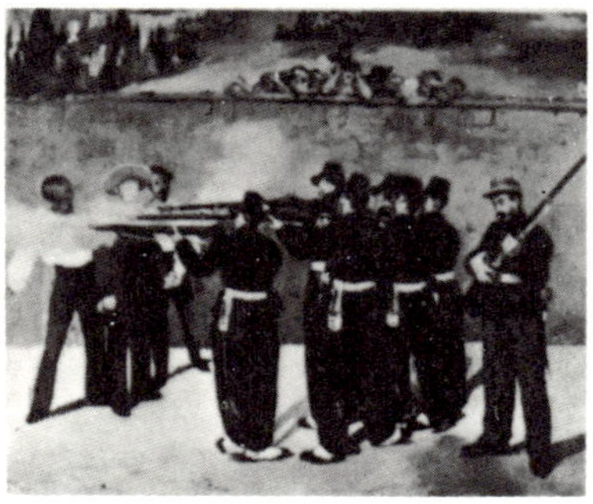

16. The Execution of Maximilian - 1867. Städtische Kunsthalle, Mannheim - *In his portrayal of an execution, Manet was looking for a negation of tragedy. The depersonalized brutality of the incident is underscored by the indifference of the soldier on the far right carefully examining his rifle. For political reasons, this canvas was not allowed to be exhibited.*

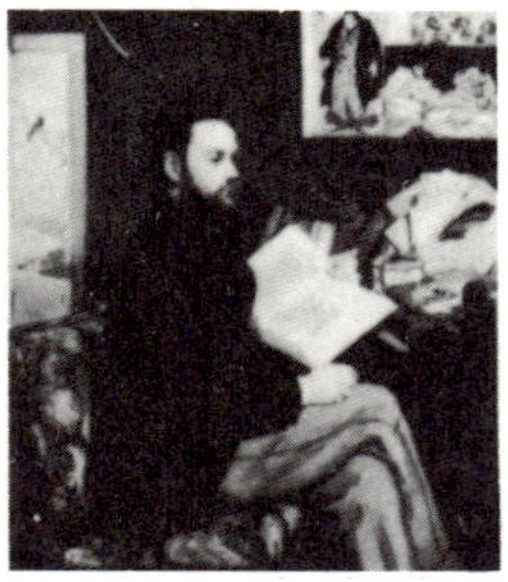

17. Portrait of Emile Zola - 1868. Musée d'Orsay, Paris - *As a mark of gratitude to Zola who had so warmly come to his defence, Manet portrayed the writer among his books and familiar objects: a Japanese screen, a print by Utamaro, and reproductions of "Olympia" and Velasquez's "The Wine-Drinkers". Manet modernised this traditional humanist portrait by painting it with a lack of expression on the writer's face.*

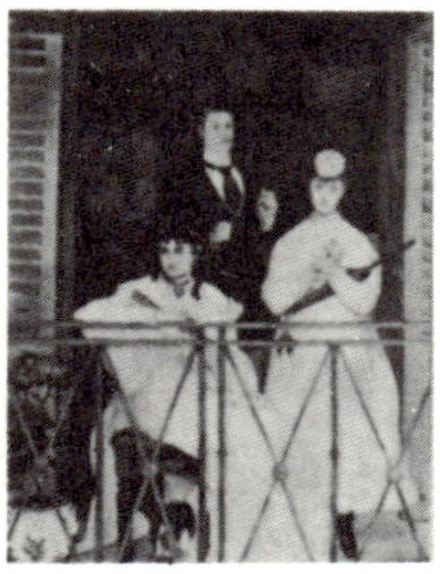

18. The Balcony - 1868-69. Musée d'Orsay, Paris - *In the middle of the composition sits Berthe Morisot, at the left the violinist Fanny Clause, and behind them, the landscape-painter Guillemet. In the shadows is Leon Leenhoff, Manet's son. In this scene, Manet has completely rejected any depth or background. The figures seem flat; there is no perspective to the painting. Of the picture, someone wrote that with the green shutters, Manet had dropped to the level of a house painter.*

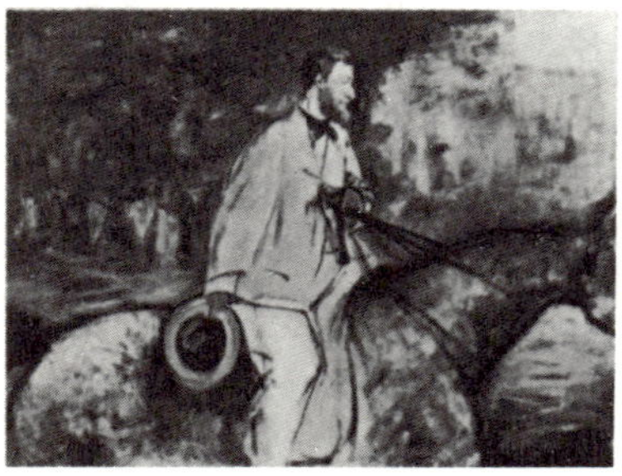

19. Portrait of Guillaudin on Horseback - 1870. Private collection, Michigan - *The long brushstrokes give a gentle contour to the figure; the background becomes a light smudge, reflecting the movement of the man on horseback. The sketch-like effect of this canvas suggests that it is unfinished.*

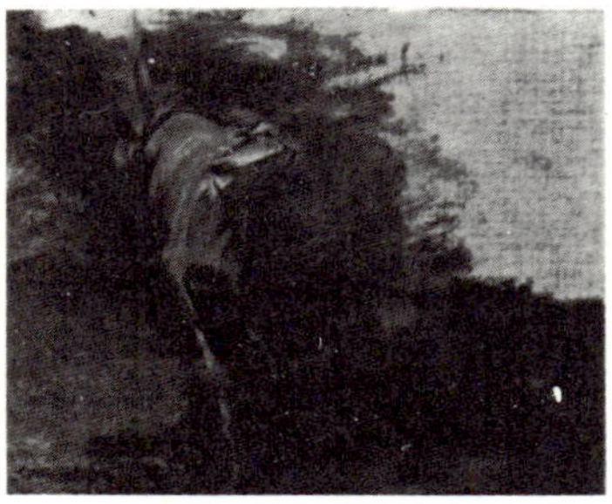

20. The Greyhound - 1871. Private collection - *A few colours and tones are all that are necessary to show the agility of the running greyhound in this improvised canvas in which the right side is left almost completely blank.*

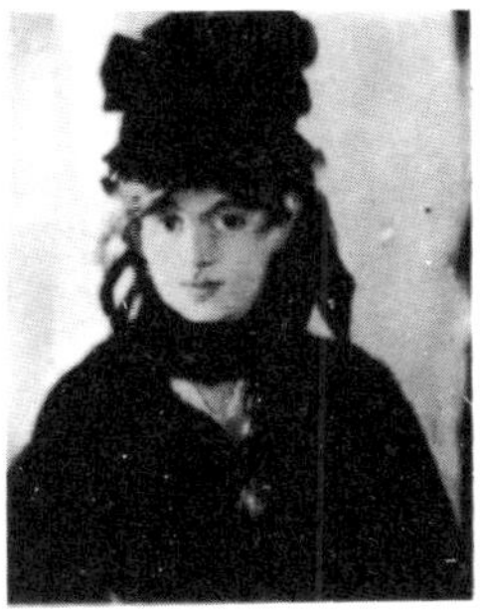

21. Berthe Morisot with a Bunch of Violets - 1872. Private collection, Paris - *Berthe Morisot, a young painting student of Corot's, would later become part of the group of Impressionists. She posed several times for Manet. In 1874 she married Eugène Manet and became Edouard's sister-in-law, and their friendship grew deeper and richer over time.*

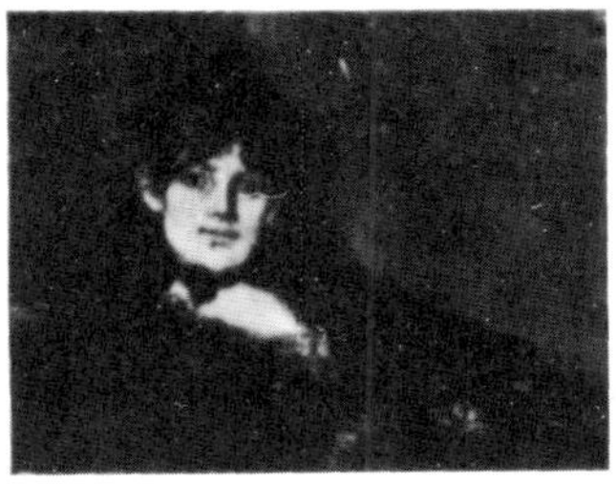

22. Portrait of Berthe Morisot reclining - 1872. Private collection, Paris - *Manet continued to paint the face and languorous attitude of Berthe Morisot for many years. The painter eliminated the lower part of the canvas as he felt he had got the perspective wrong.*

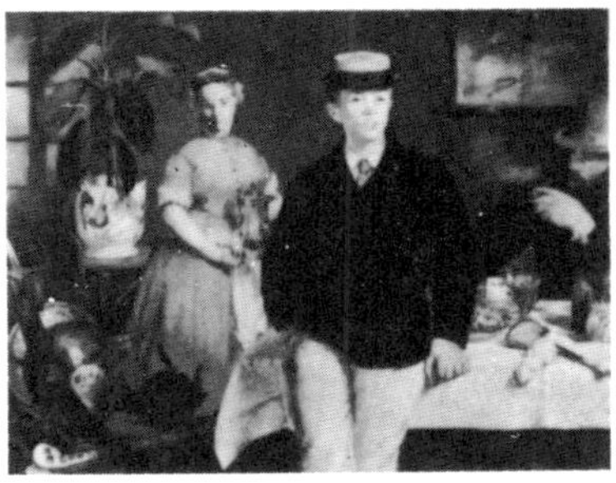

23. Lunch in the Studio - 1868. Bayerische Staatsgemälde Sammlungen, Munich - *The figures and objects have a singular force in this painting. The young man in the foreground is Léon Leenhoff, of whom Manet was officially the guardian. It is on him that the painter has concentrated his attention, and especially on the anticipation that his face communicates to the other figures.*

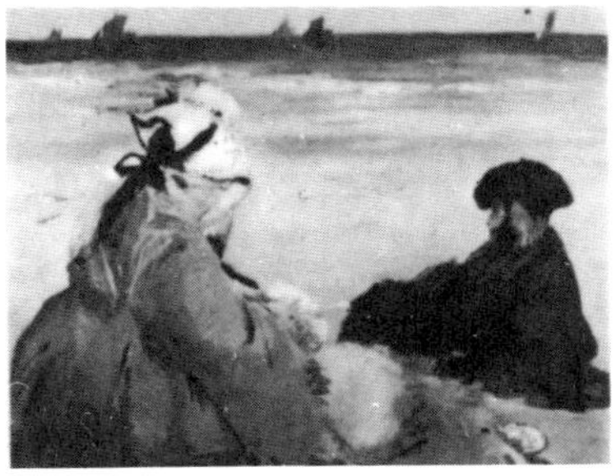

24. On the Beach at Boulogne - 1873. Musée d'Orsay, Paris - *This canvas, painted in Boulogne where Manet often stayed in summer, has a luminous transparent quality to it. At the time, Manet's interest in painting outdoors was growing stronger.*

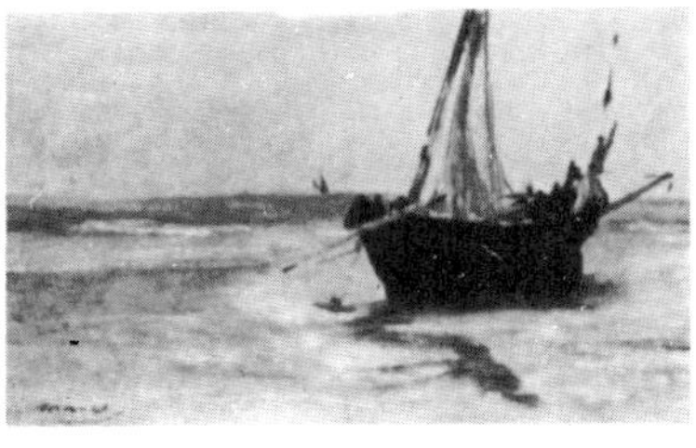

25. The Black Boat at Berck - 1873. Private collection - *Manet painted several seascapes. Contemplating the sea allowed him to use beautiful flat tones of colour in the Japanese manner. The sea seemed to the painter like a flat surface on top of which the boat rested.*

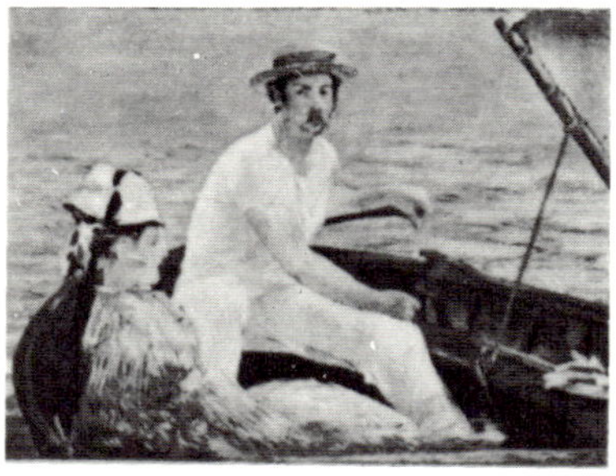

26. The Boat - 1874. Metropolitan Museum of Art, New York - *The light tones, the canvas painted outdoors, the point of view set high so that the horizon blocks the background, the use of a scene from everyday life, all combine to make this a true Impressionist painting. Manet, who had been the leader of a school of painting, has here submitted to the influence of Monet and Renoir.*

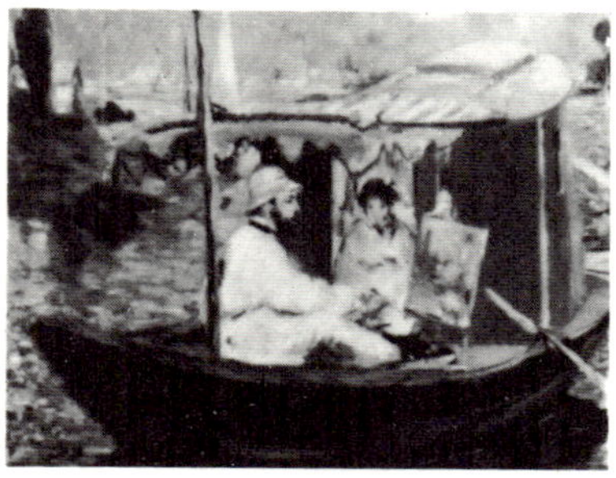

27. Monet in his Studio Boat - 1874. Neue Pinakothek, Munich - *In this old boat anchored in Argenteuil, Monet painted and received his friends. The banks of the Seine inspired the Impressionist painter to study light. He often moved about looking for new motifs, drifting down the river so dear to Parisians.*

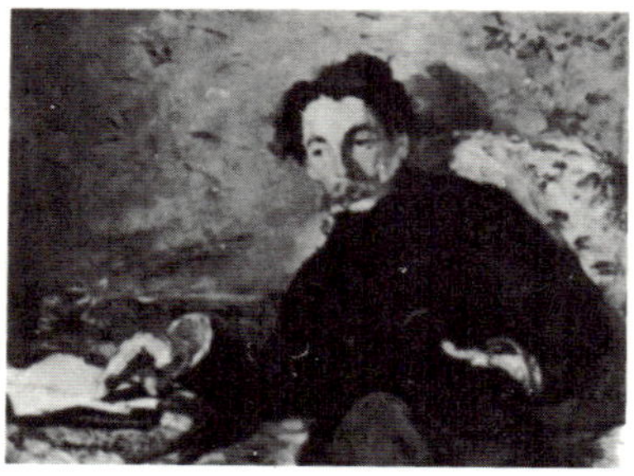

28. Portrait of Stéphane Mallarmé - 1876. Musée du Louvre, Paris - *A deep friendship, coupled with a rich intellectual exchange of ideas, linked Manet and Mallarmé for many long years. If the portrait of Zola was stripped of emotional content, this portrait represents Manet's evolution, for now he tried to let the character of his sitter shine through, so that even the hands of the poet express tension.*

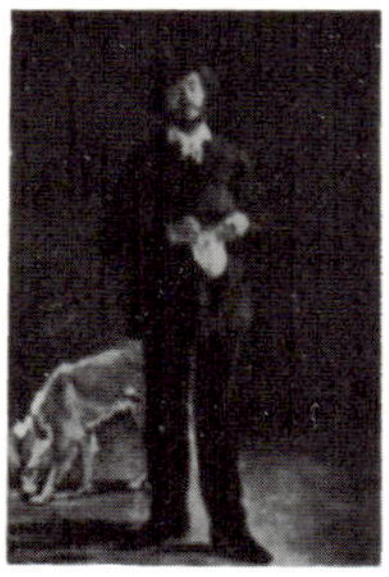

29. The Artist - 1875. Museu de Arte, São Paulo - *This is a portrait of Mercellin Desboutin, a messy unrestrained dabbler in paint. This painting was rejected by the jury of the Salon of 1876 along with "The Laundress".*

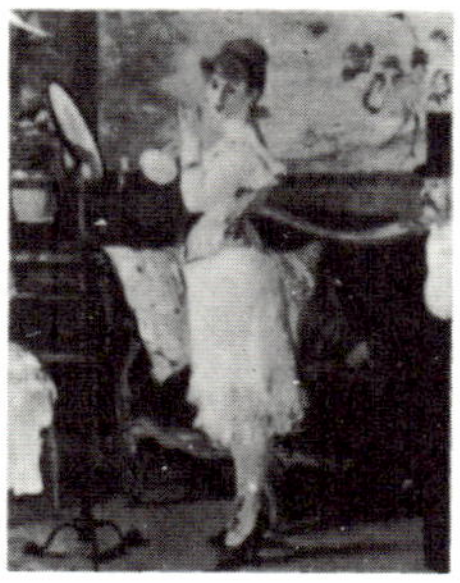

30. Nana - 1877. Kunsthalle, Hamburg - *In 1877, in the windows of the publishers Giroux, boulevard des Capucines, one could see this canvas, rejected by the Salon. This scene of the world of the "demi-monde", considered vulgar at the time, recalls the naturalistic atmosphere of that world, one which Manet was certainly not unaware of, and even more, it suggests the easy life that would later be described by Guy de Maupassant.*

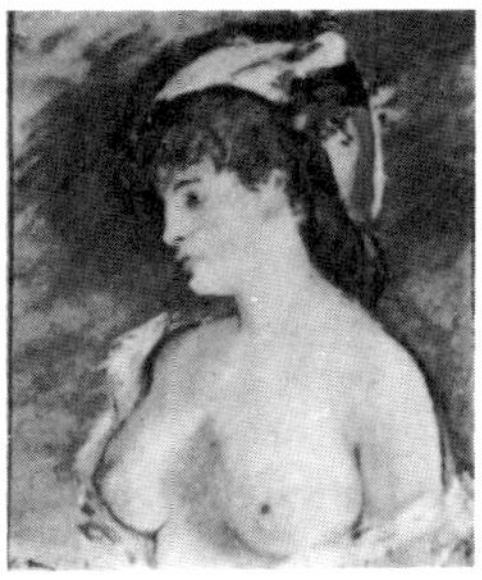

31. Blonde Semi-nude - 1875. Musée du Louvre, Paris - *The brushstrokes in this painting seem almost caressing. The canvas is sparsely covered with thick paint spread on in zones, with white and reddish-ochre touches giving a sensual feeling to the figure. The sombre tones of "Brunette Semi-nude" give way here to lighter colours.*

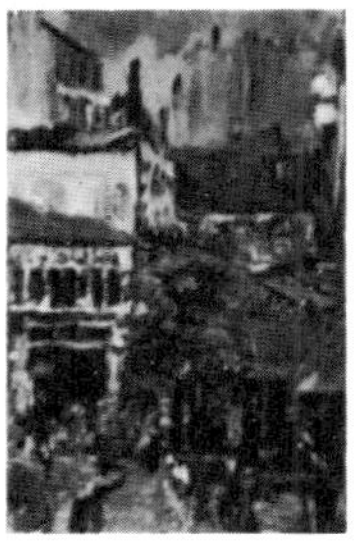

32. View from near the Place Clichy - 1875-78. Private collection - *With a virtuosity of palette, Manet employs a vast range of colours in this work with which the artist communicates not only forms, proportions, and depth but also suggests the state of his own soul.*

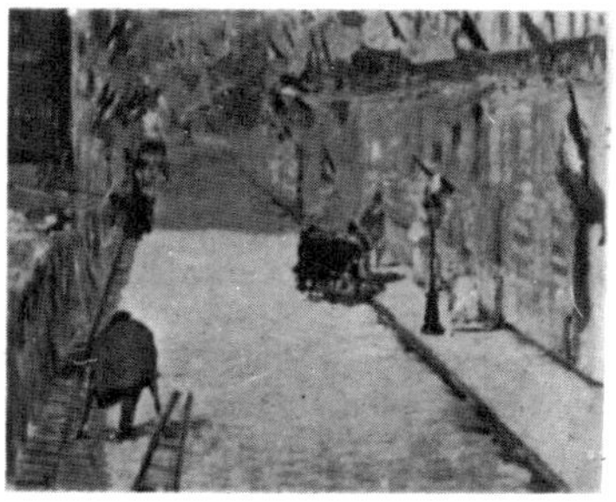

33. Rue Mosnier Decked with Flags - 1878. Private collection, Virginia - *To celebrate the Universal Exhibition of 1870, June 30th was declared a national holiday and banners were hung all over the city. Manet, like many other artists, wanted to catch on canvas the chromatic richness of the decked-out streets.*

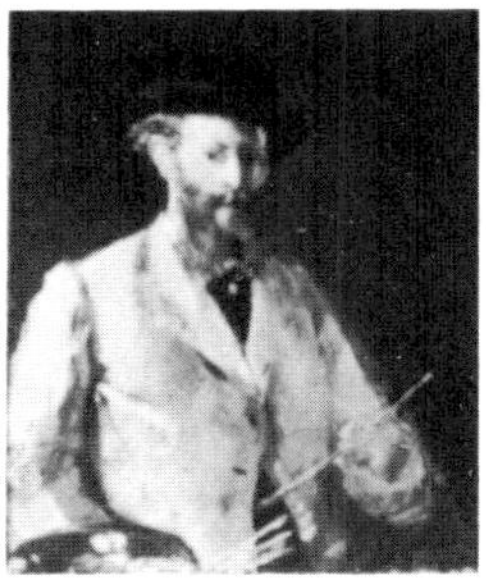

34. Self-Portrait - 1879. Private collection, New York - *Manet painted this self-portrait when he was 47, and with a sense of humour showed himself putting the last touches of colour on his yellow jacket. As in the portrait of Mallarmé, his hand betrays emotion.*

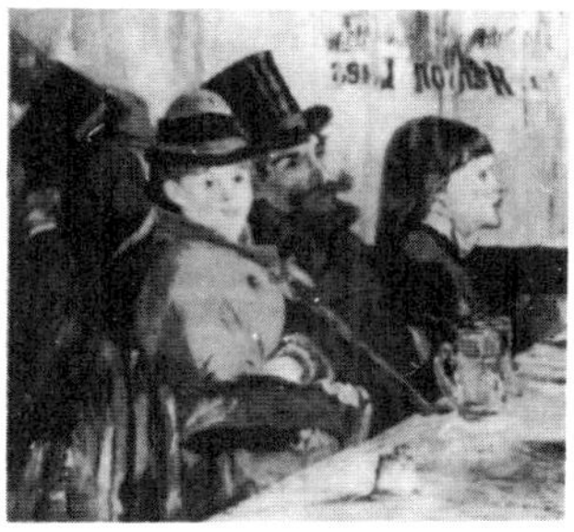

35. At the Café - 1878. O. Reinhart am Roemerholz Collection, Winterthur - *Manet, the painter of modern life, Manet, the boulevardier and sophisticate, loved to visit and paint cafés with their brilliant cheerful atmosphere. A typical situation like this became for him a chance to paint a scene from everyday life.*

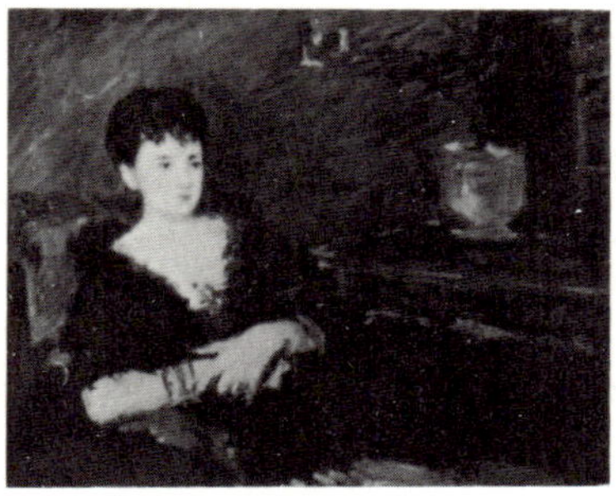

36. Isabelle Lemonnier, seated - 1878-79. Private collection - *If one compares these portraits with those of his early years, one can see that in spite of the Impressionist characteristics of the canvas, the painter continued to use the contrasts of black and white that made his paintings so vigorous.*

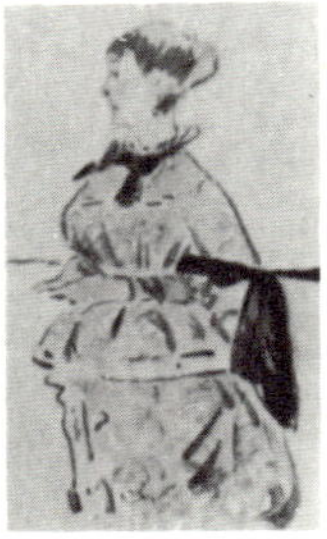

37. Isabelle Lemonnier - 1880. Musée du Louvre, Paris - *This was most likely an exercise by the painter to record his impressions on paper, confirmed by the rough outline of the figure and the transparency of colour.*

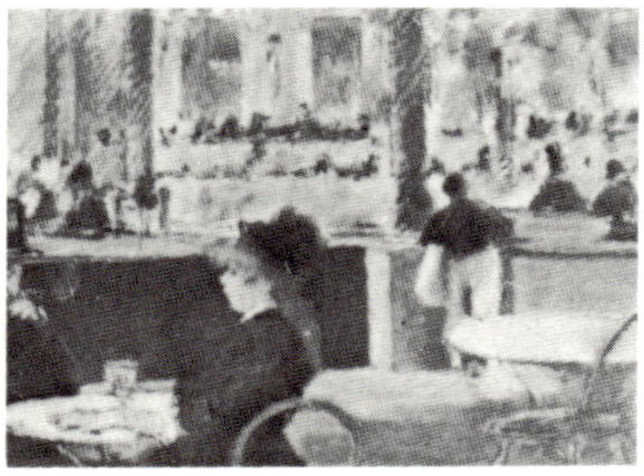

38. The Café on the rue du Théâtre Français - date unknown - Burrell Collection, Glasgow. *At night a café like this was crowded with people, but during the day the place was almost empty, and the atmosphere completely different. The massive use of white contributes to create the impression of emptiness.*

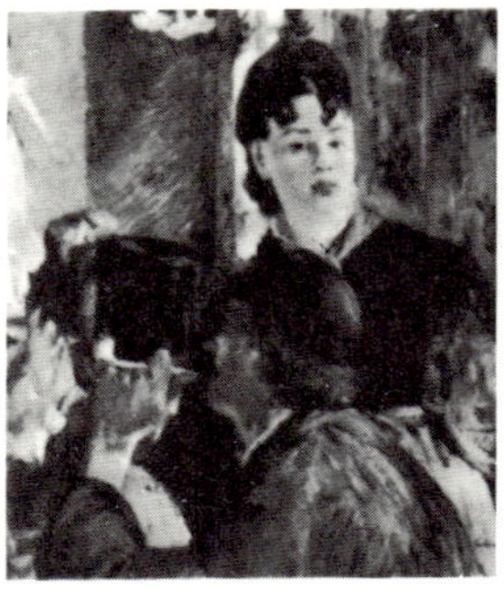

39. The Bon Bock - 1879. Musée d'Orsay, Paris - *The cabarets with their customers and their waitresses inspired Manet to paint a series of tableaux. The brasserie-café-concert "Au Cabaret de Reischoffen" with its audience of musicians, actors, and artists inspired the painter to paint this glimpse of Parisian life.*

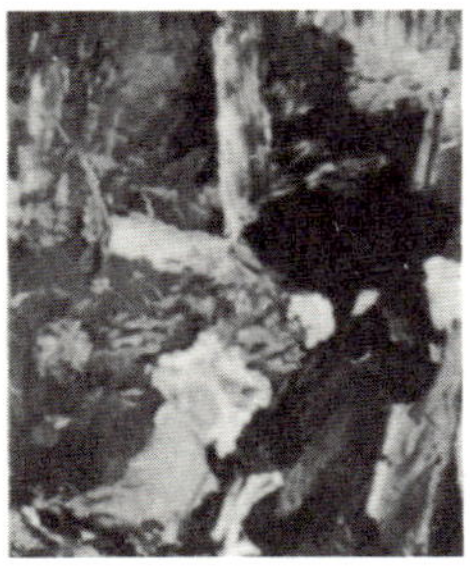

40. Manet's Mother in the Garden of Bellevue - 1880. Private collection, Paris - *Manet's mother is represented here in a particularly happy attitude. The brushstrokes are wide and confident; the accumulation of thick paint gives colour to the canvas. One can almost feel the rhythm of his mother's hands as they knit.*

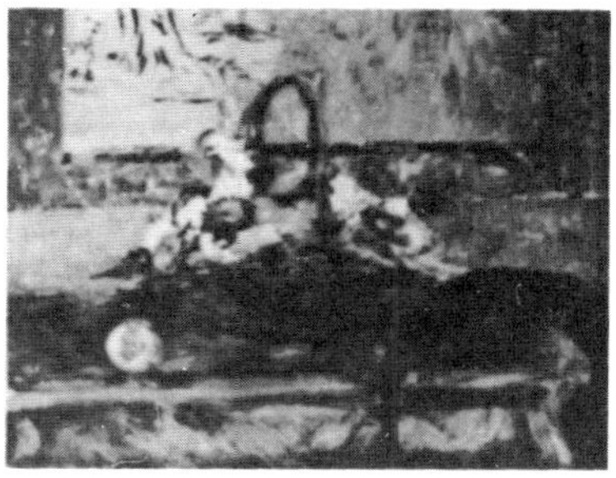

41. Basket of Flowers - 1880. Private collection - *This still-life manifests the Impressionist techniques used by Manet towards the end of his life. The richness of colour and background details are witness to the artistic evolution of the painter with regard to his earlier simpler still-lifes.*

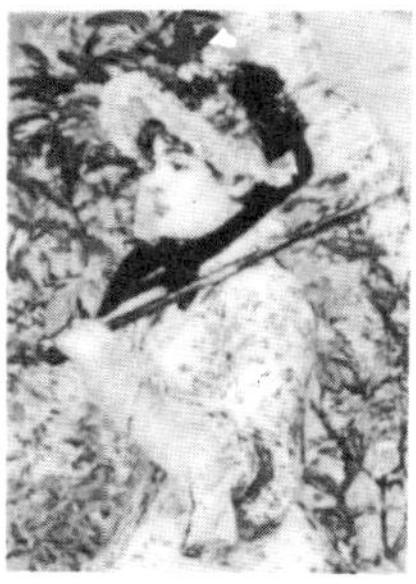

42. Spring (Jeanne de Marsy) - 1881. Private collection, New York - *By now quite ill, Manet still managed to paint the face of this pretty actress whom he had also portrayed in "Young Woman with Cloak". This work met with great success when it was shown at the last Salon in which Manet participated.*

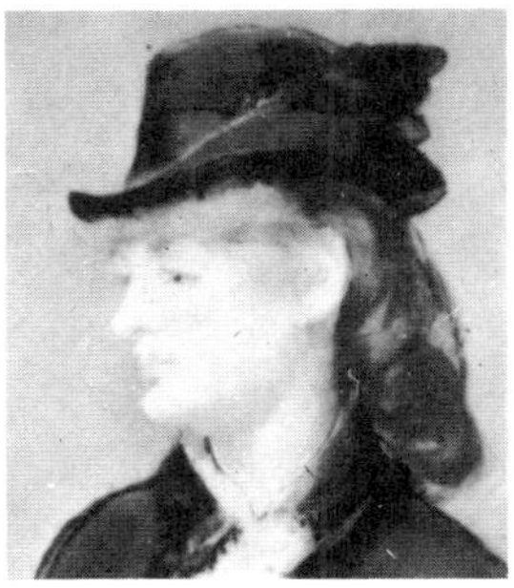

43. Model for Bar at the Folies-Bergère - 1881. Musée des Beaux-Arts, Dijon - *Suzon, the waitress at the bar of the Folies-Bergère, posed for this delicate pastel. At the end of his life, Manet, who by now suffered relentless pain, used this technique almost exclusively because it did not require any great effort to achieve the effect he was looking for.*

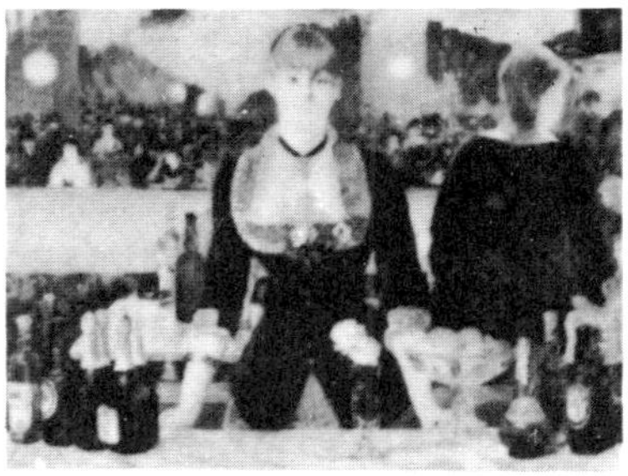

44. Bar at the Folies-Bergère - 1881-82. Courtauld Institute Galleries, London - *Manet was able to paint this work during a moment when his illness was in remission. The burst of colours and the brilliance of the gas lamps reflected in the mirrors, crystal, and bottles creates an almost unreal atmosphere, expressing the ephemerality of the pleasures of the night. This work was enormously successful.*

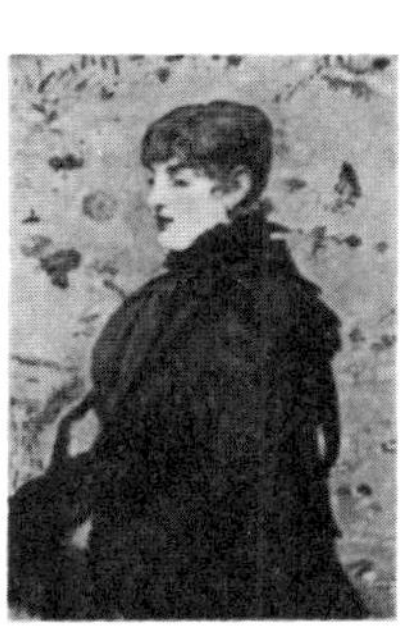

45. Autumn (Méry Laurent) - 1881-82. Musée des Beaux-Arts, Nancy - *Manet conceived the idea of painting the four seasons using four different models, but summer and winter were never painted. Méry Laurent, who had genuine affection for the artist, was the inspiration for several portraits.*

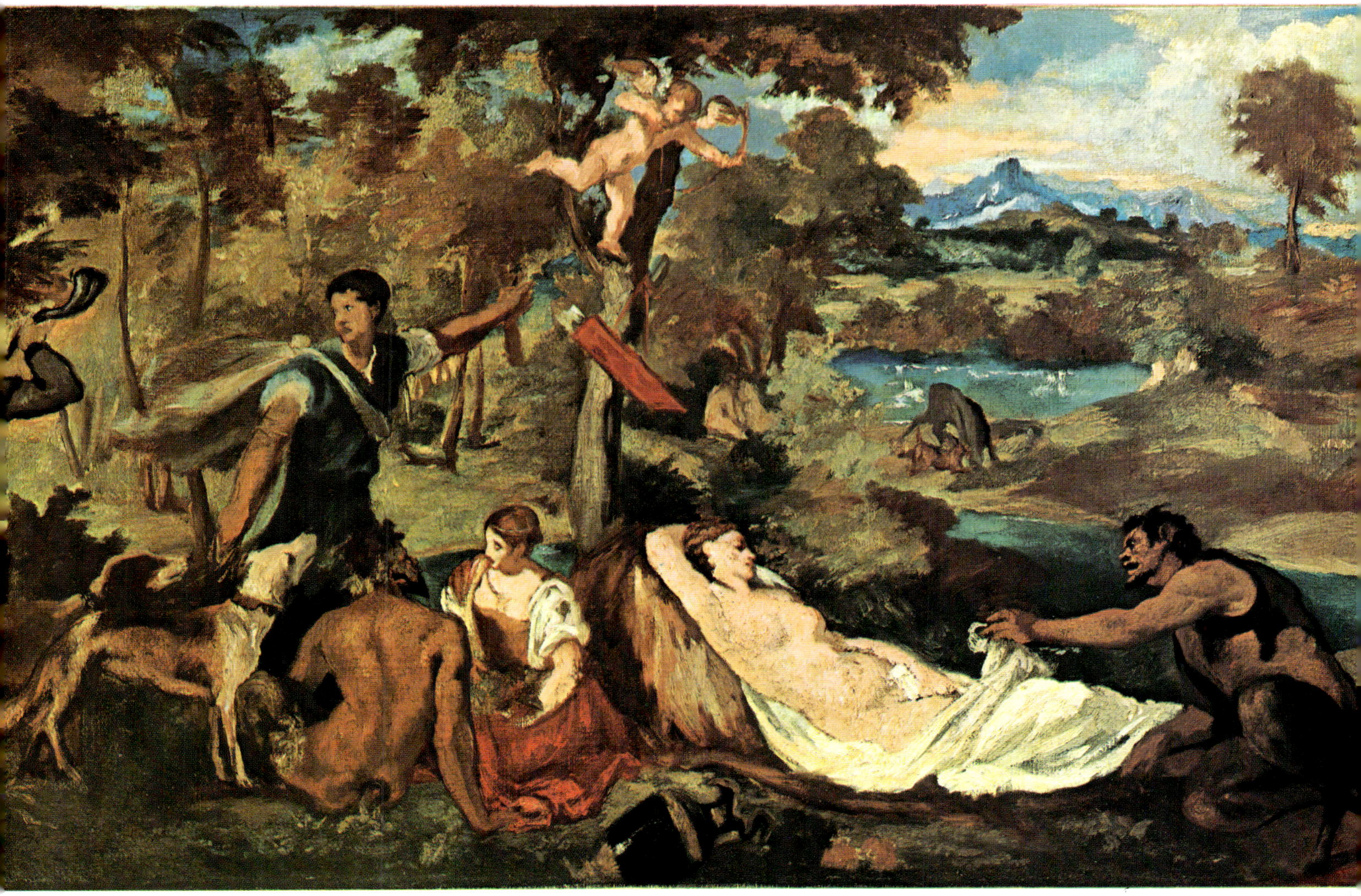

1. *Jupiter and Antiope* - 1856. Private collection, Paris

2. *Portrait of Mr. and Mrs. Auguste Manet* - 1860. Musée d'Orsay, Paris

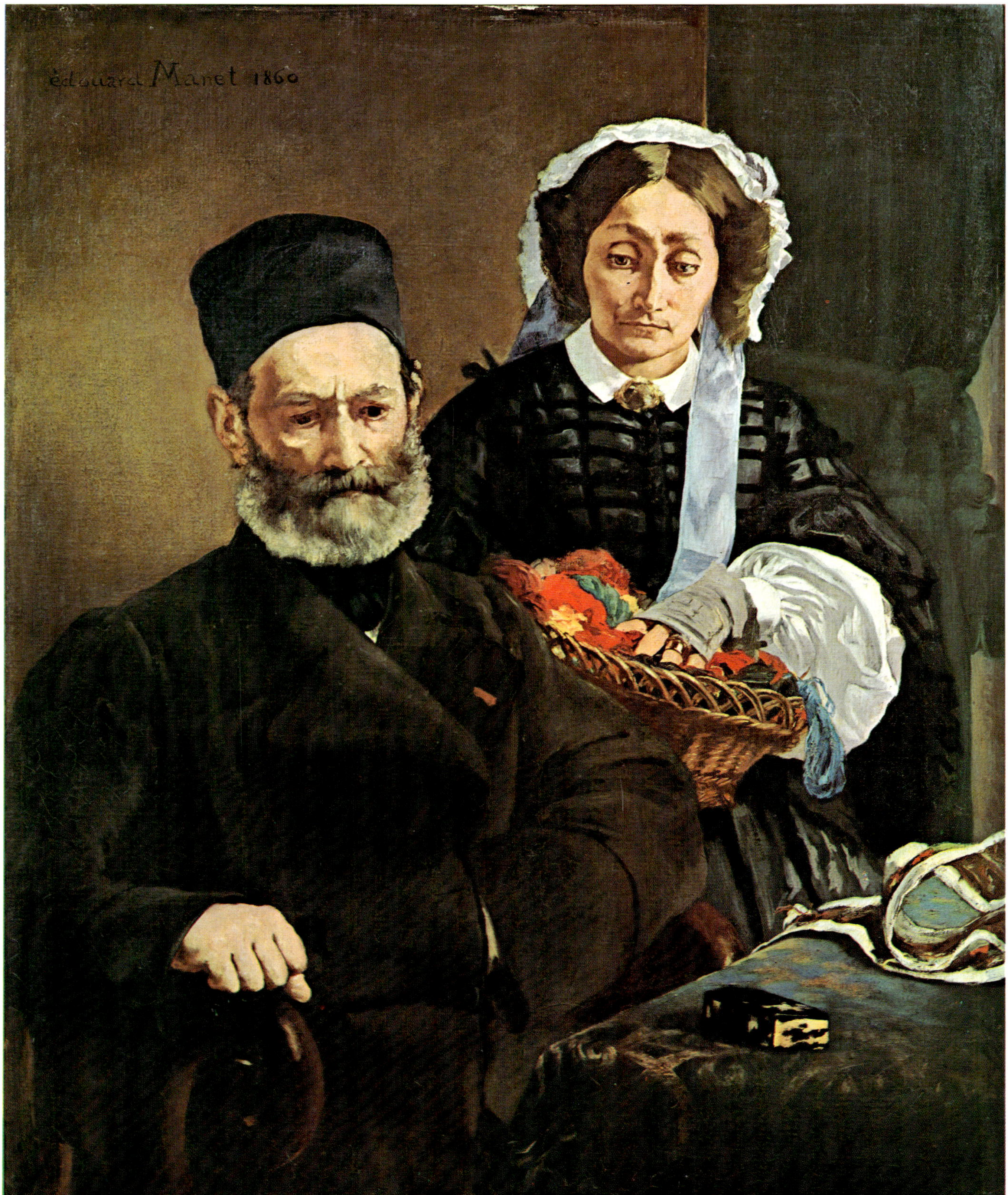

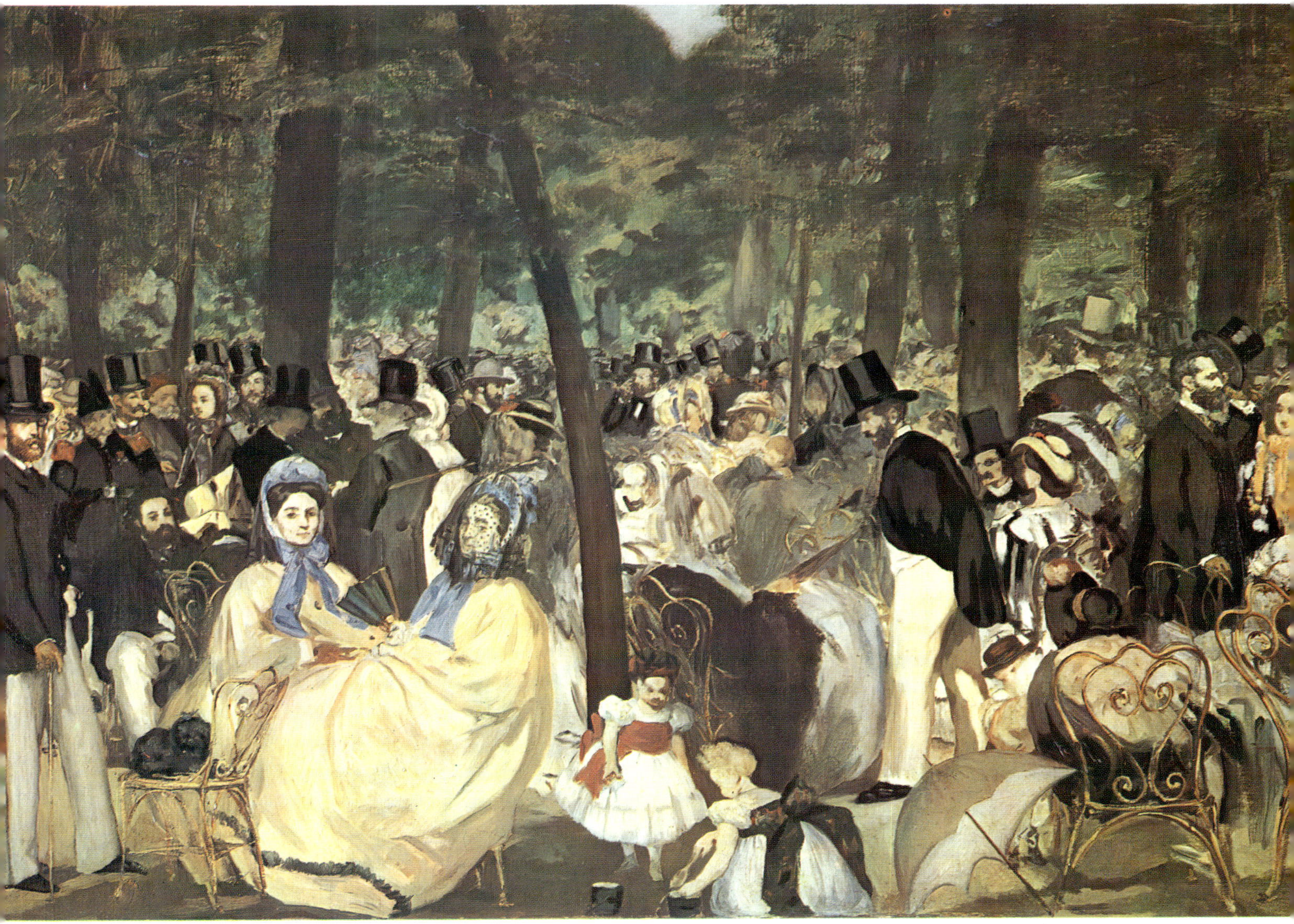

3. *Concert in the Tuileries* - 1862. National Gallery, London

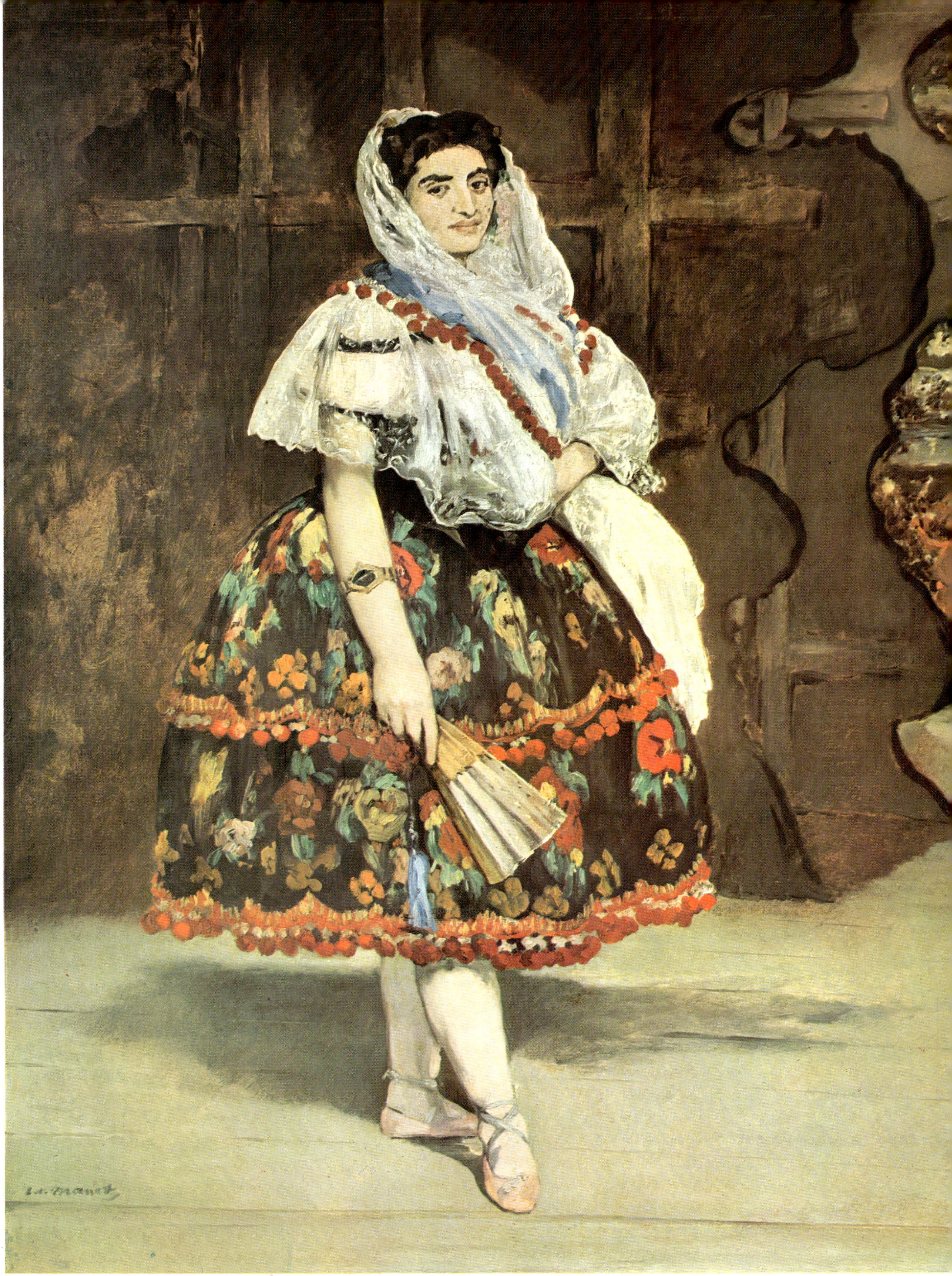
Ed. Manet

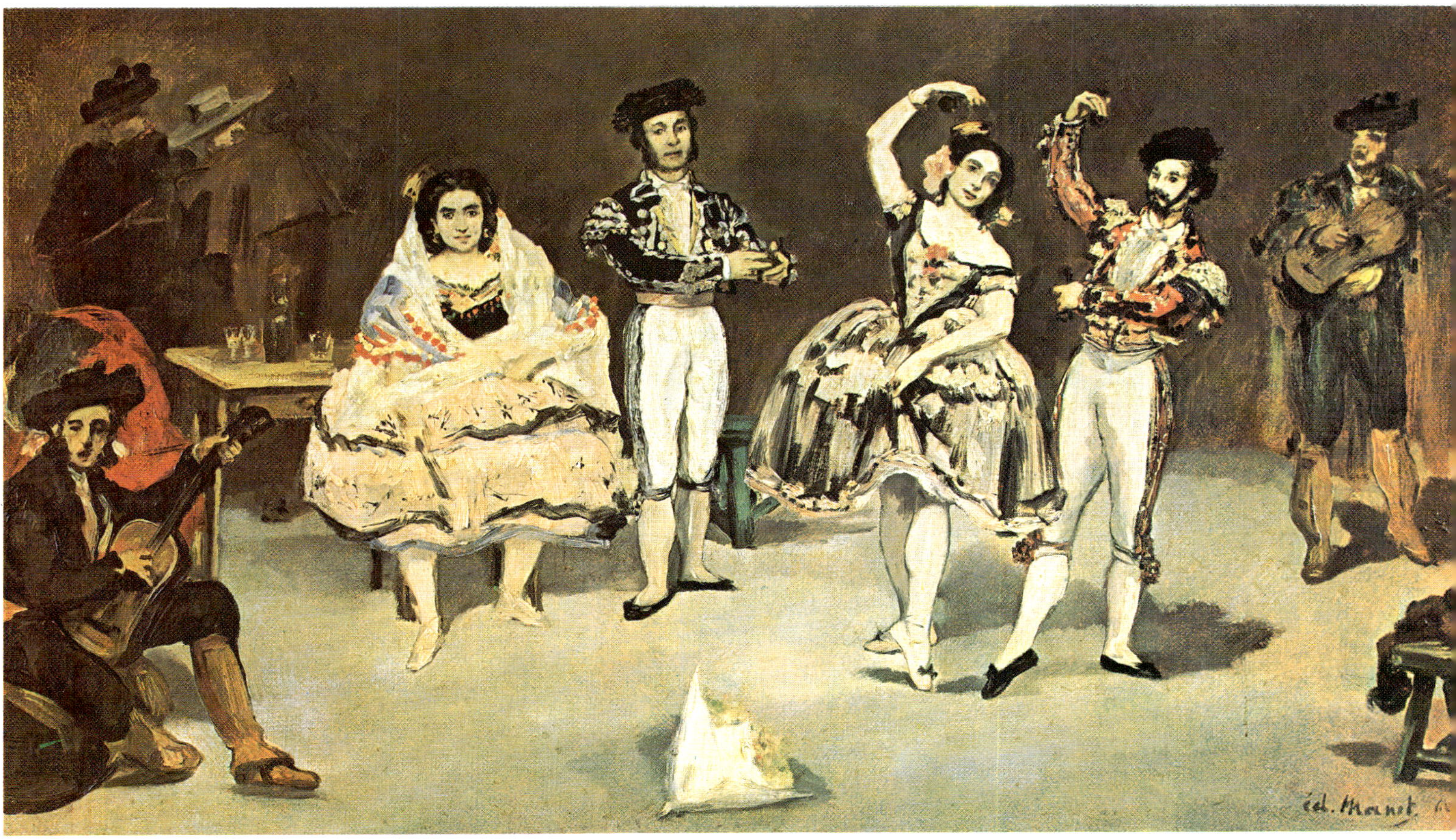

5. *Spanish Dancers* - 1862. Phillips Collection, Washington, D.C.

4. *Lola de Valence* - 1862. Musée du Louvre, Paris

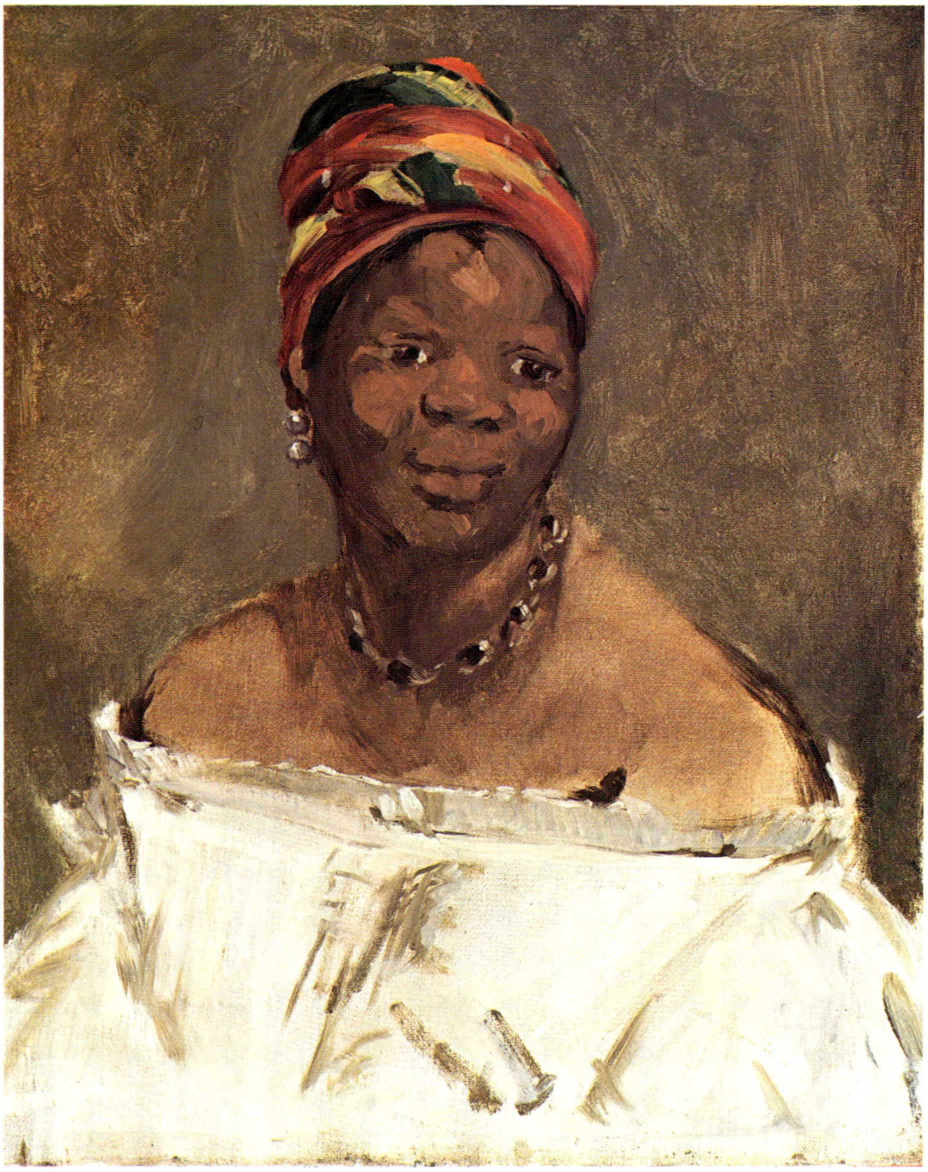

6. *The Negress* - 1863. Private collection

7. *Olympia* - 1863. Musée d'Orsay, Paris

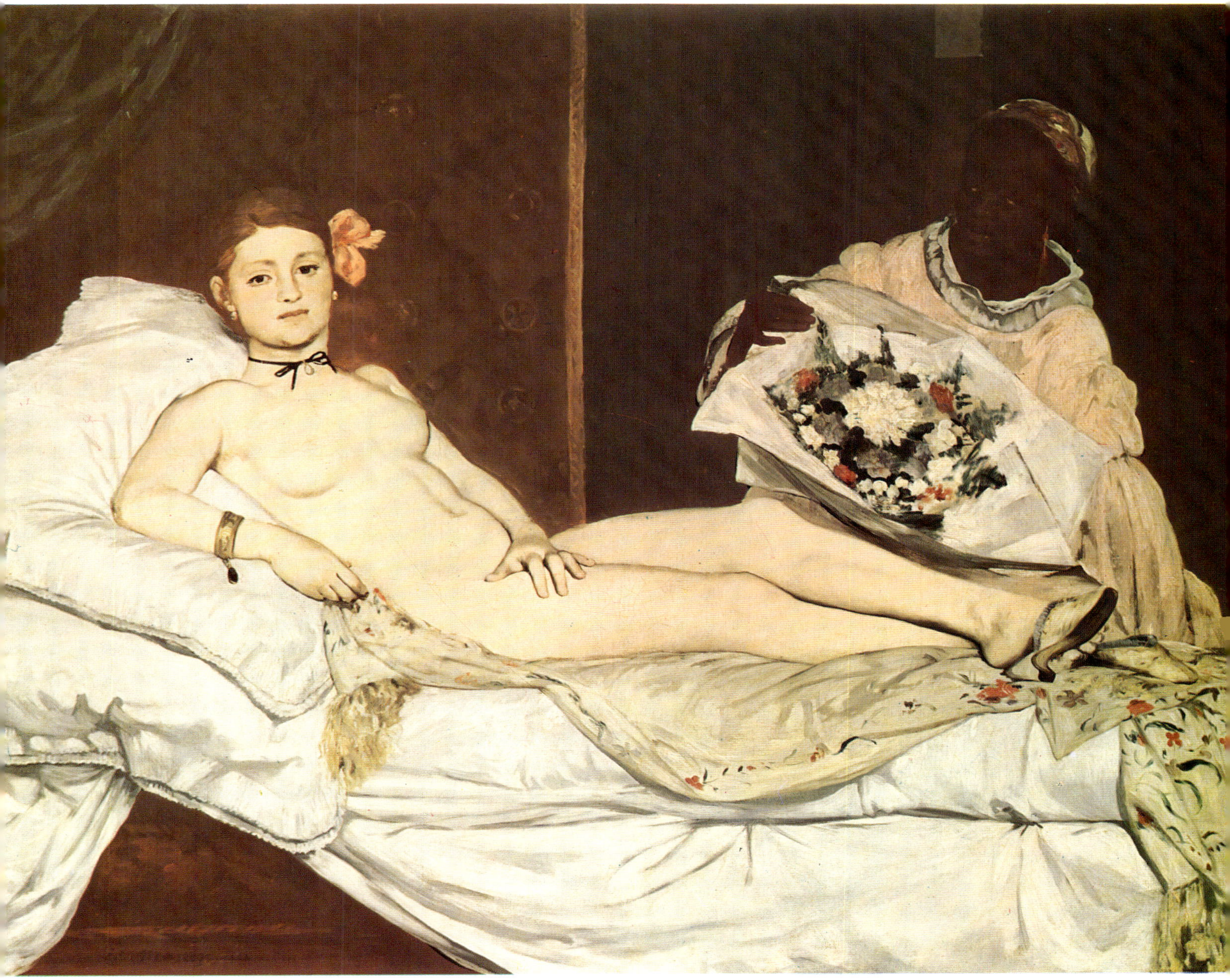

8. *Luncheon on the Grass* - 1863. Musée d'Orsay, Paris

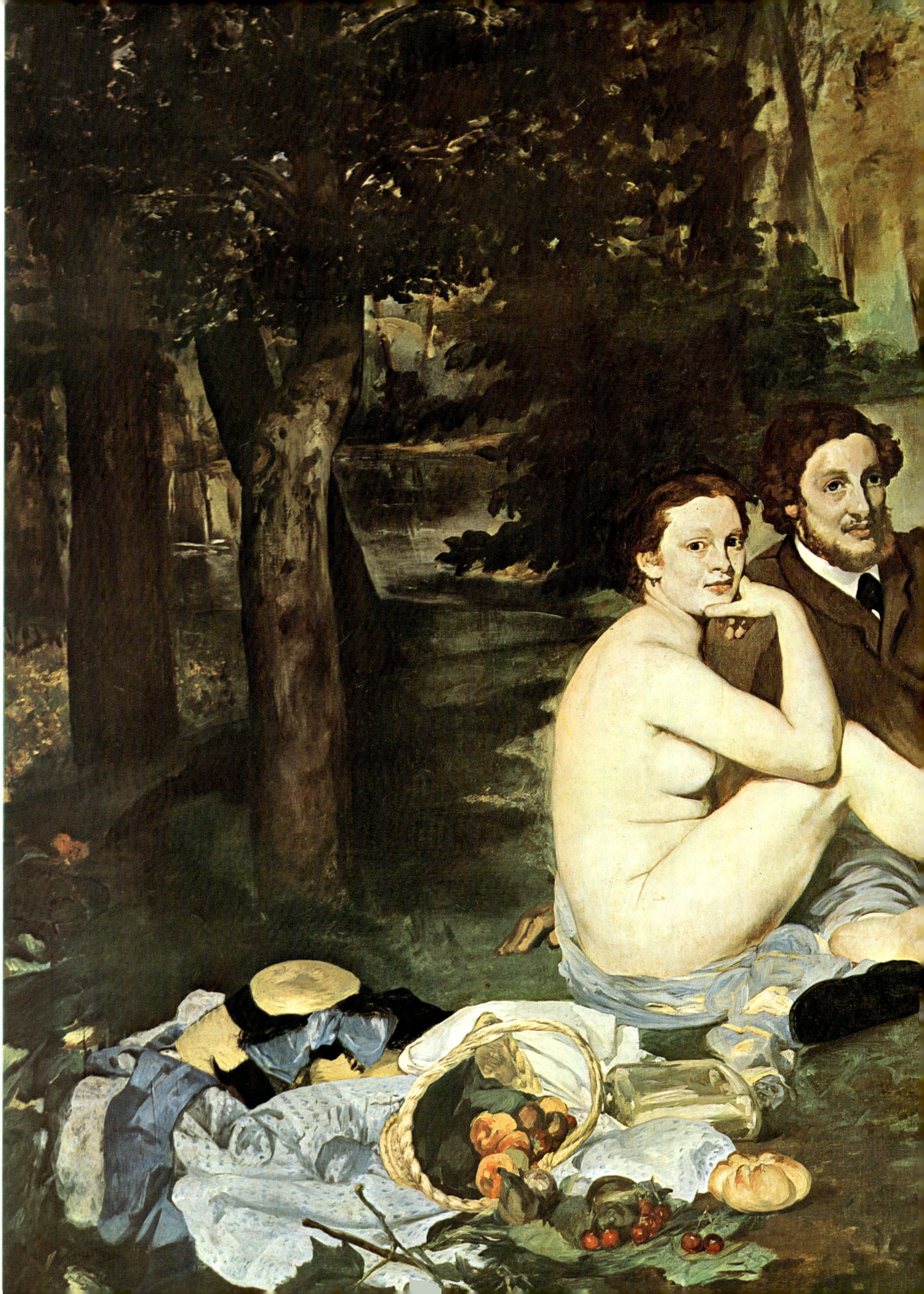

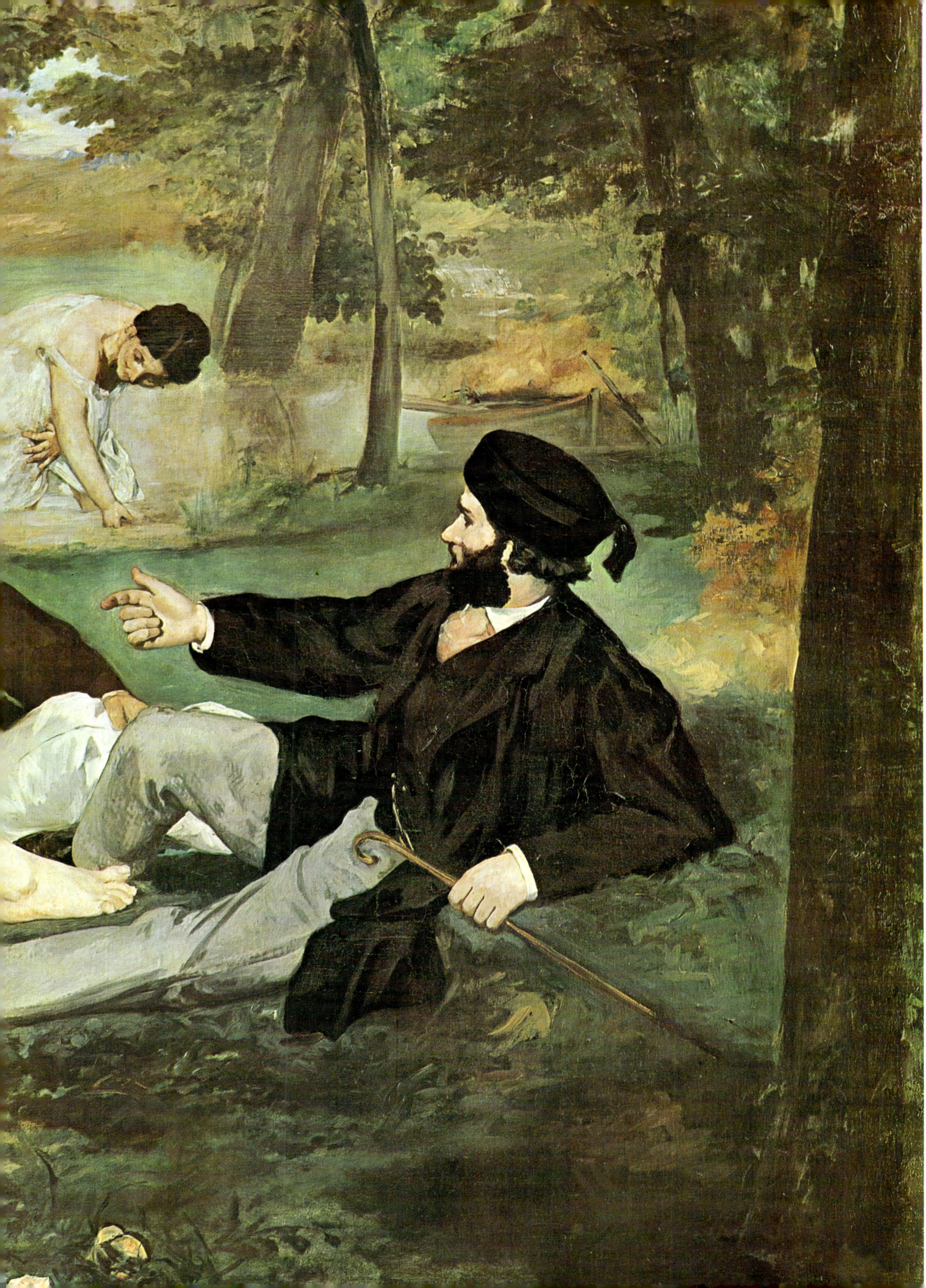

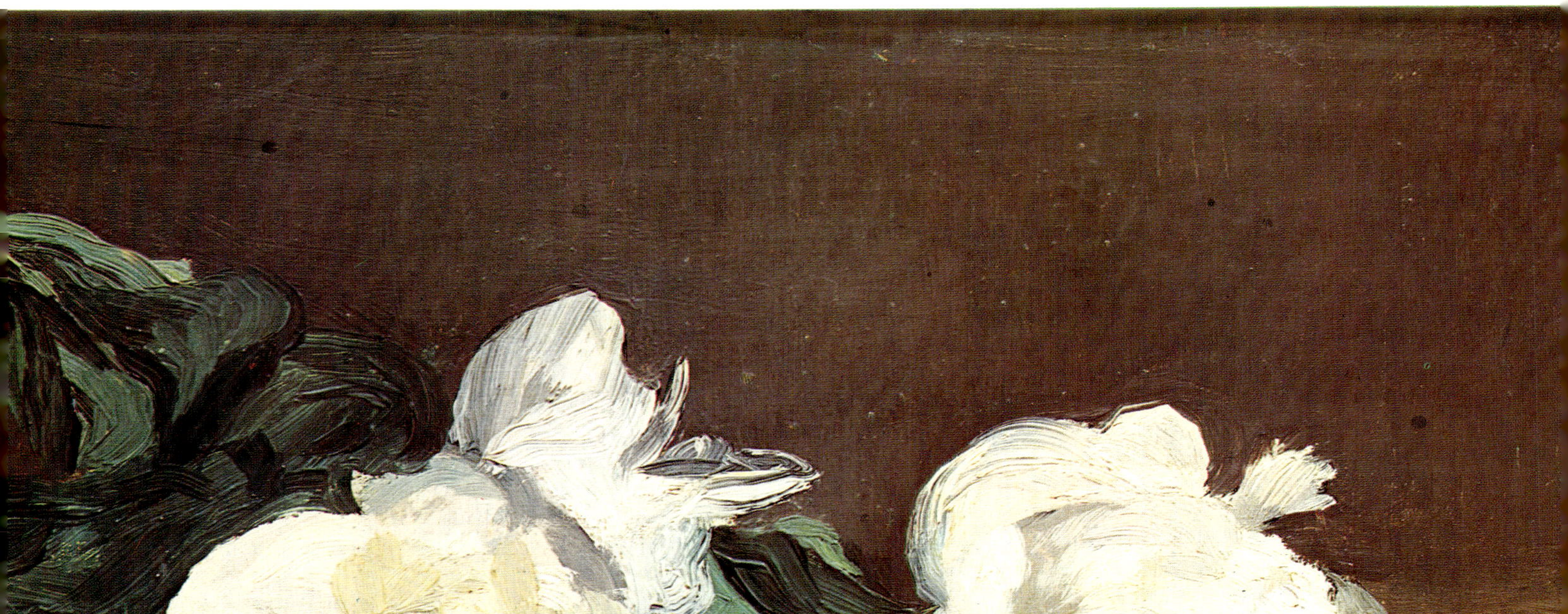

9. *Bunch of Peonies and Pruning Scissors* - 1864. Musée du Louvre, Paris

10. *Peonies with Scissors* - 1864. Musée du Louvre, Paris

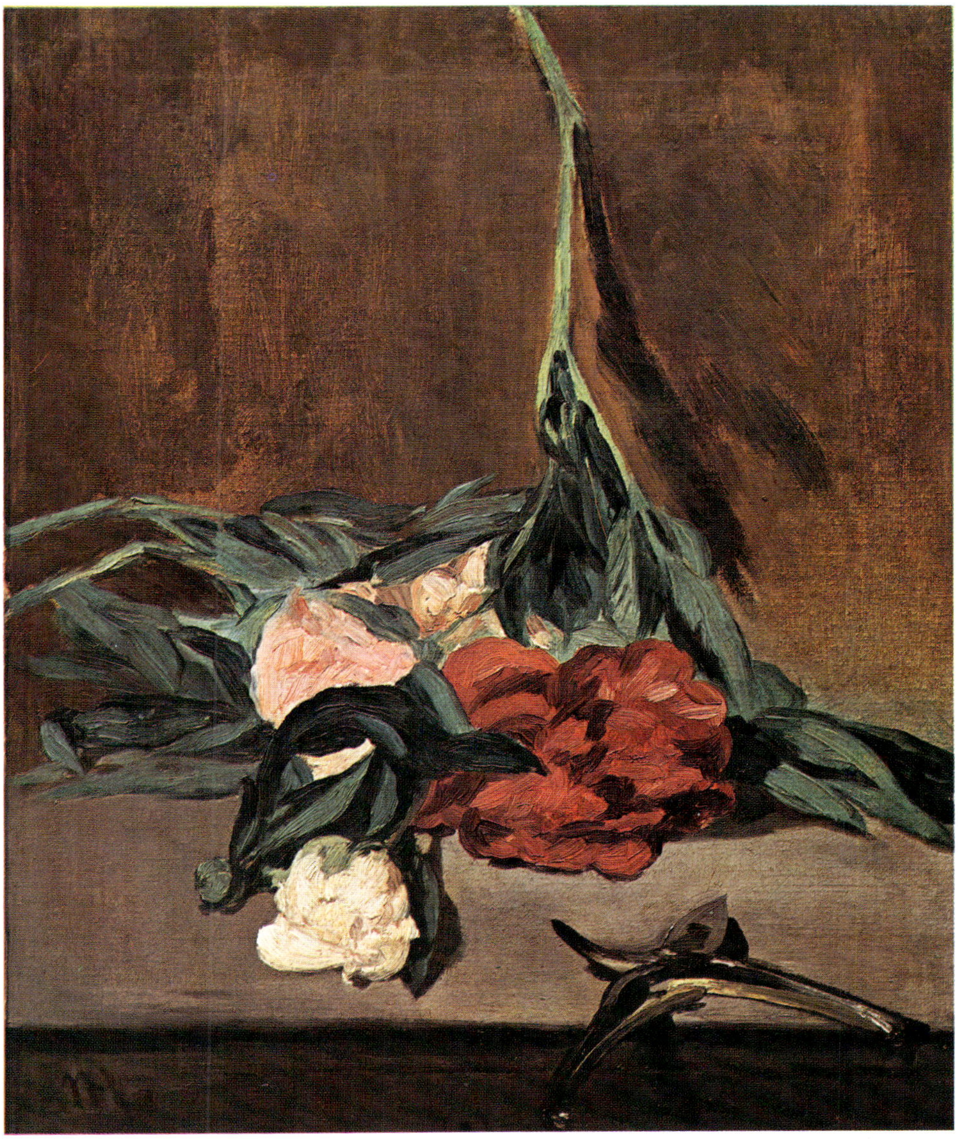

11. *Vase of Peonies* - 1864. Musée du Louvre, Paris

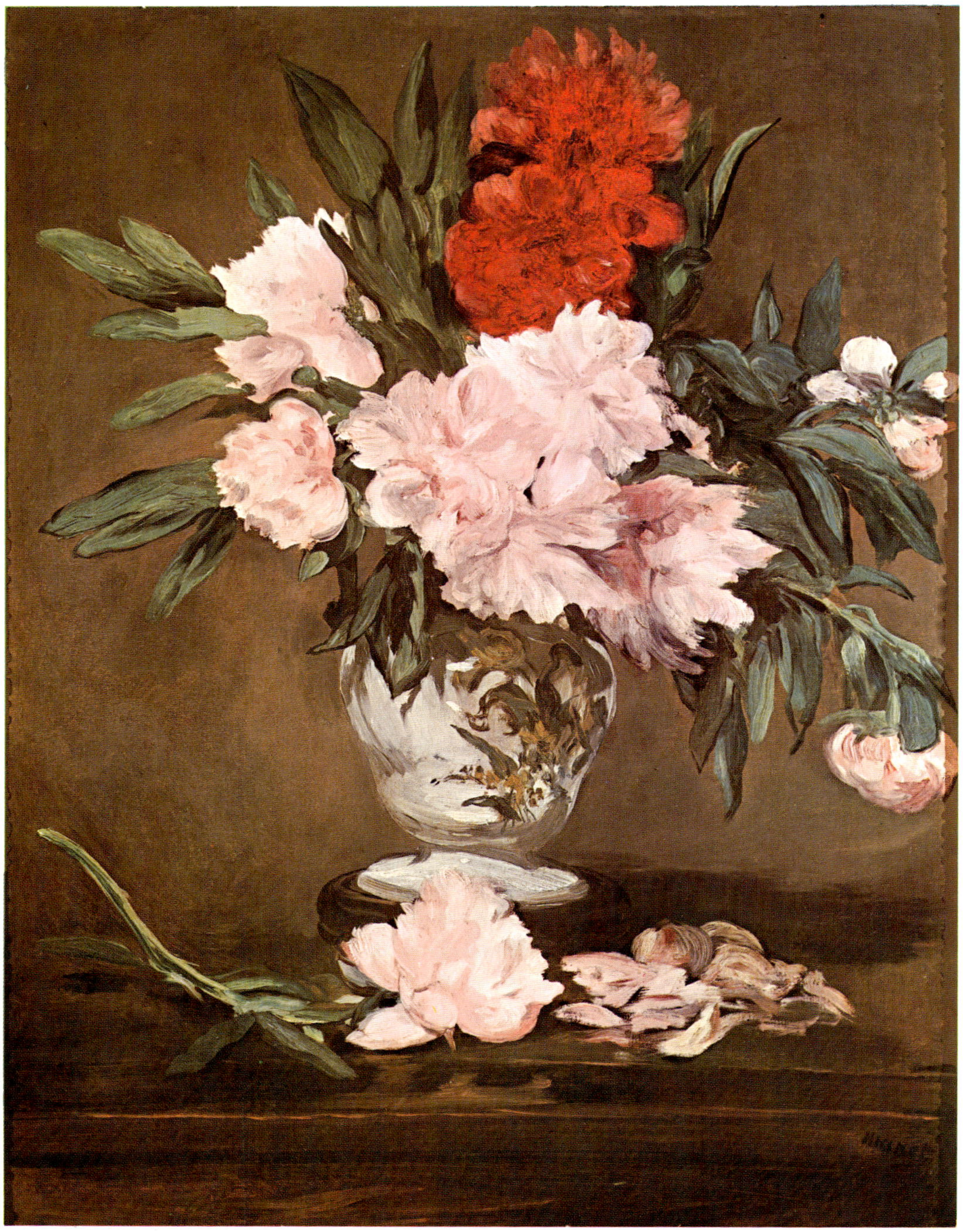

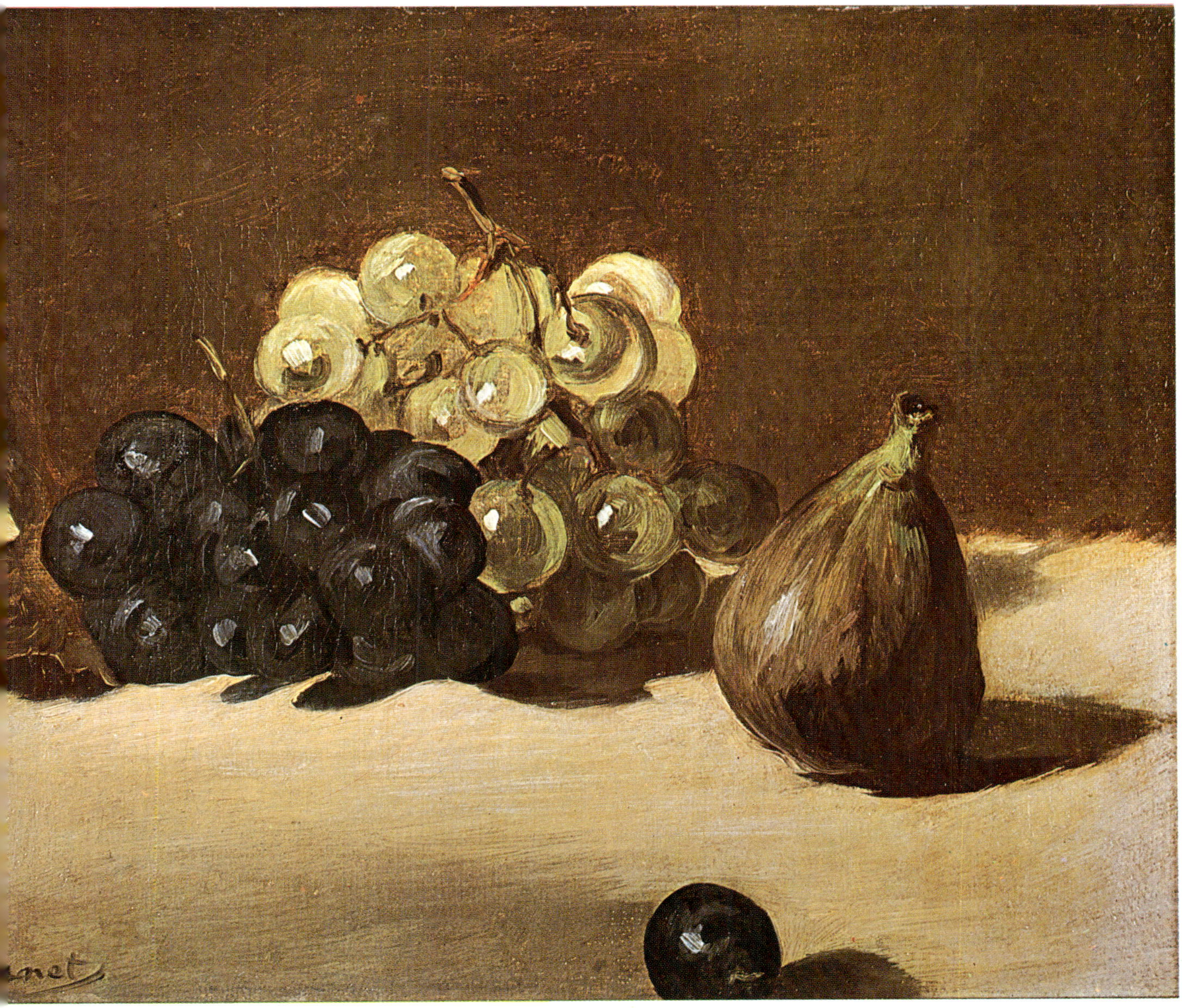

12. *Grapes and Figs* - 1864. Mrs Florence Gould Collection, Cannes

13. *The Dead Toreador* - 1864. National Gallery of Art, Washington, D.C.

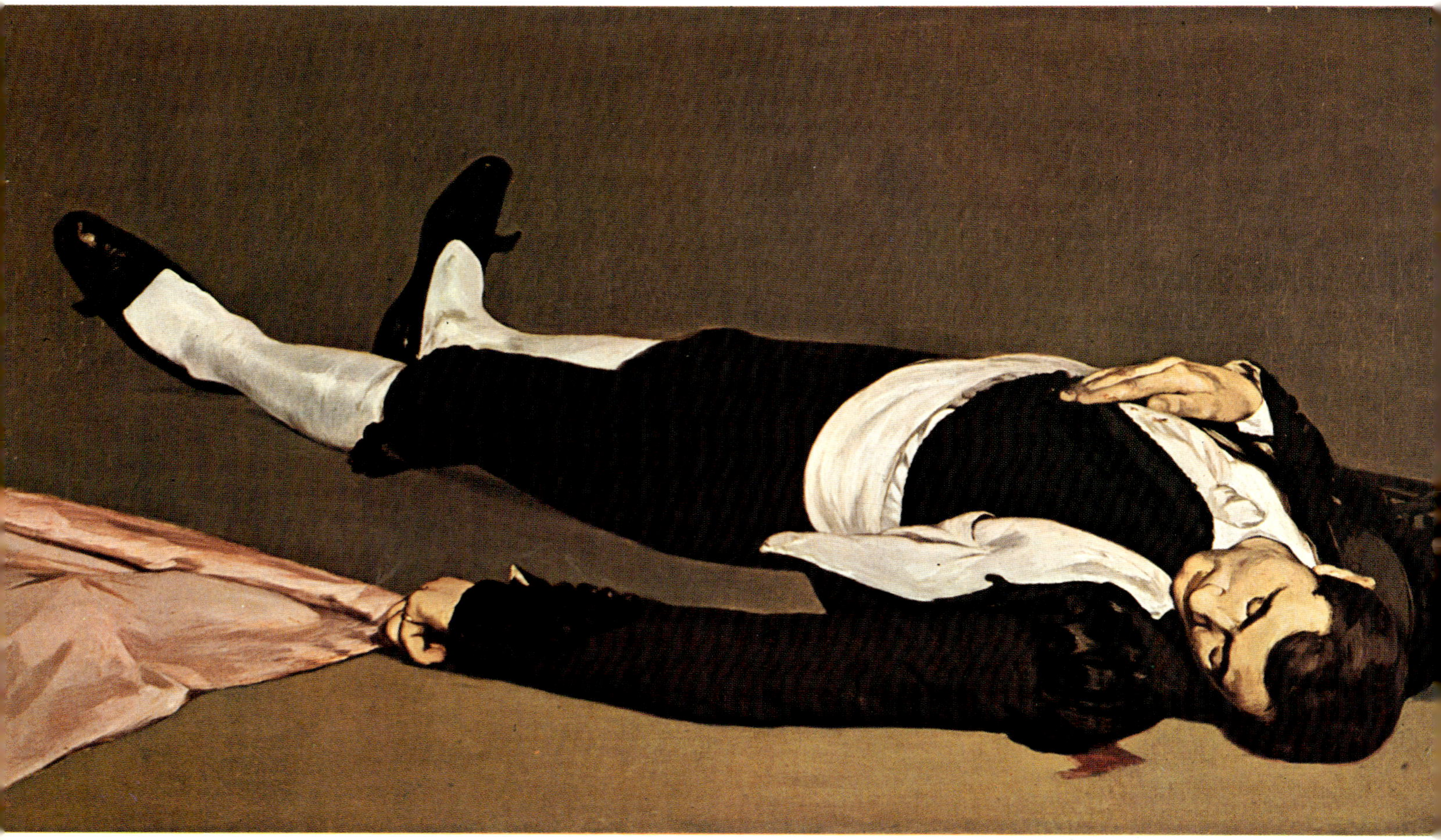

14. *The Fifer* - 1866. Musée d'Orsay, Paris

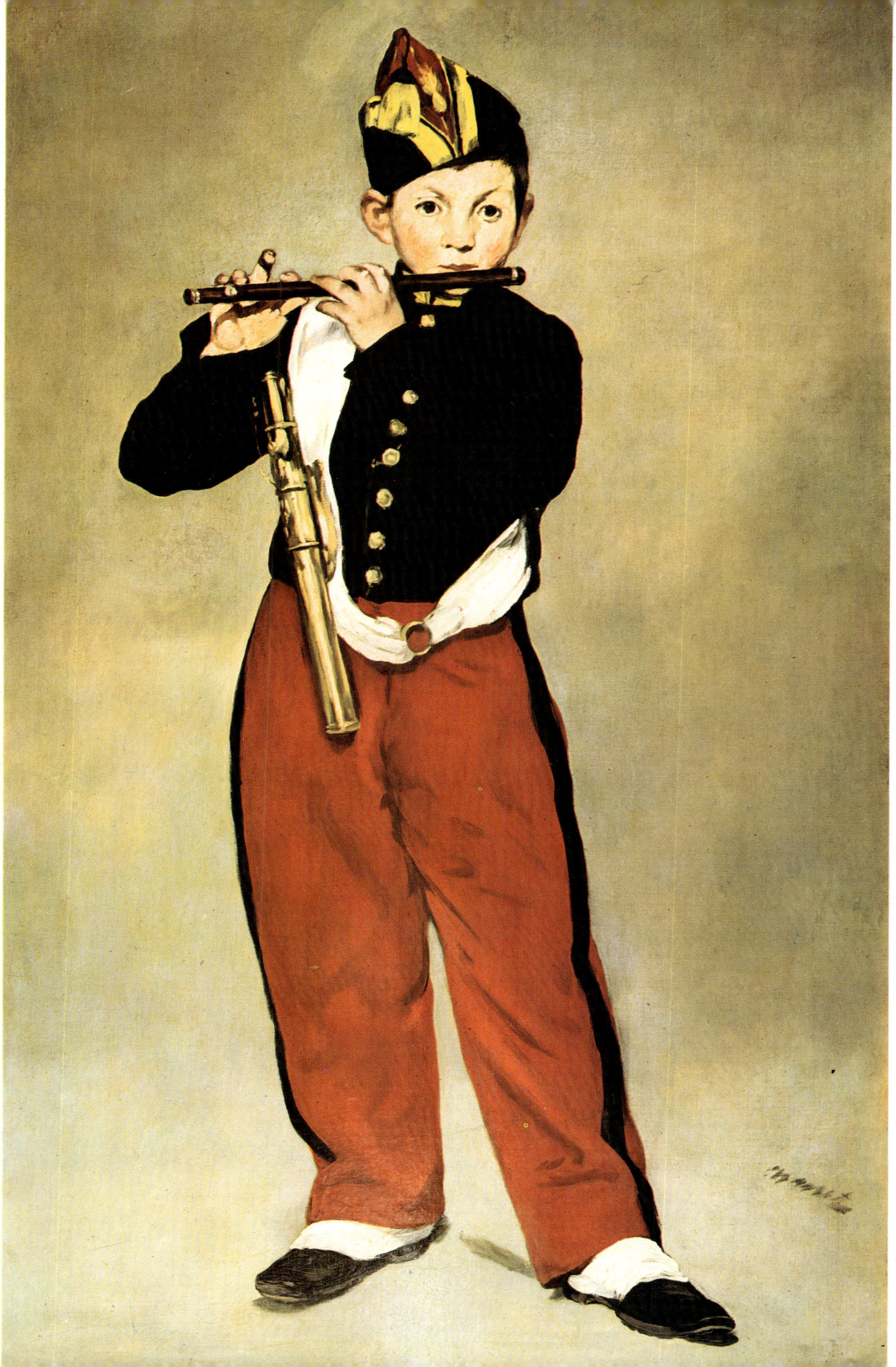

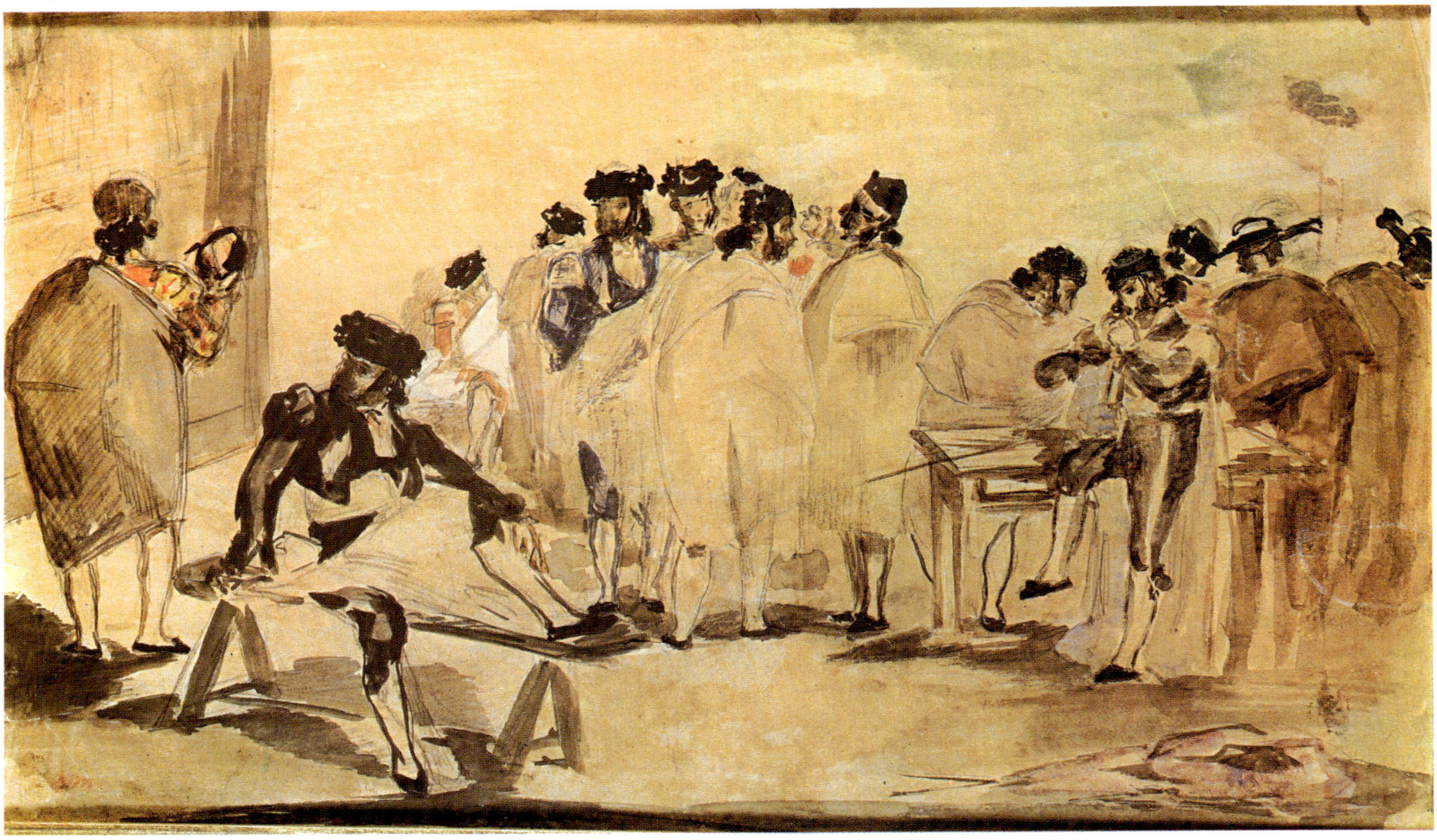

15. *The Bullfighters* - 1865-66. Hill-Stead Museum, Connecticut

16. *The Execution of Maximilian* - 1867. Städtische Kunsthalle, Mannheim

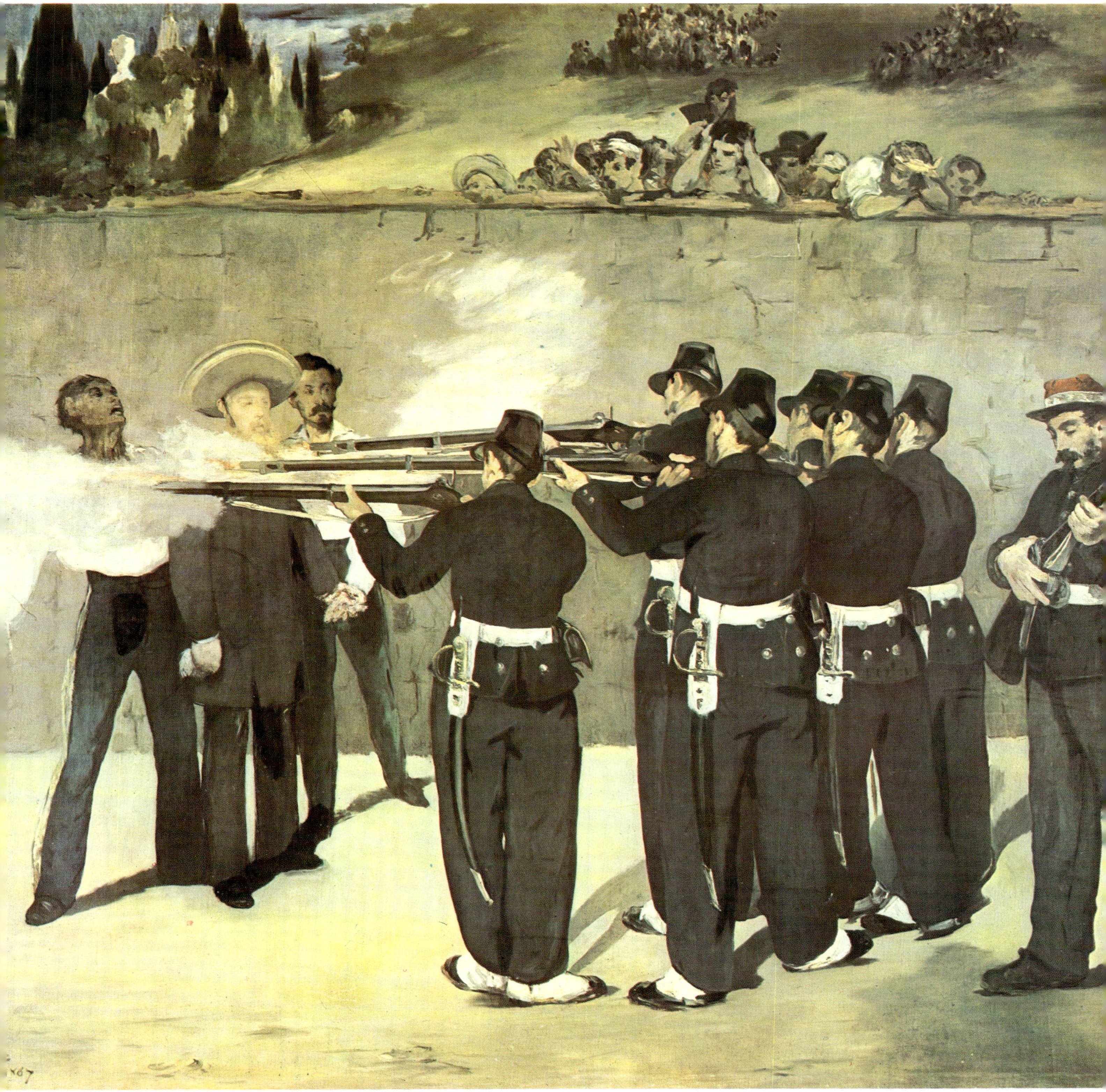

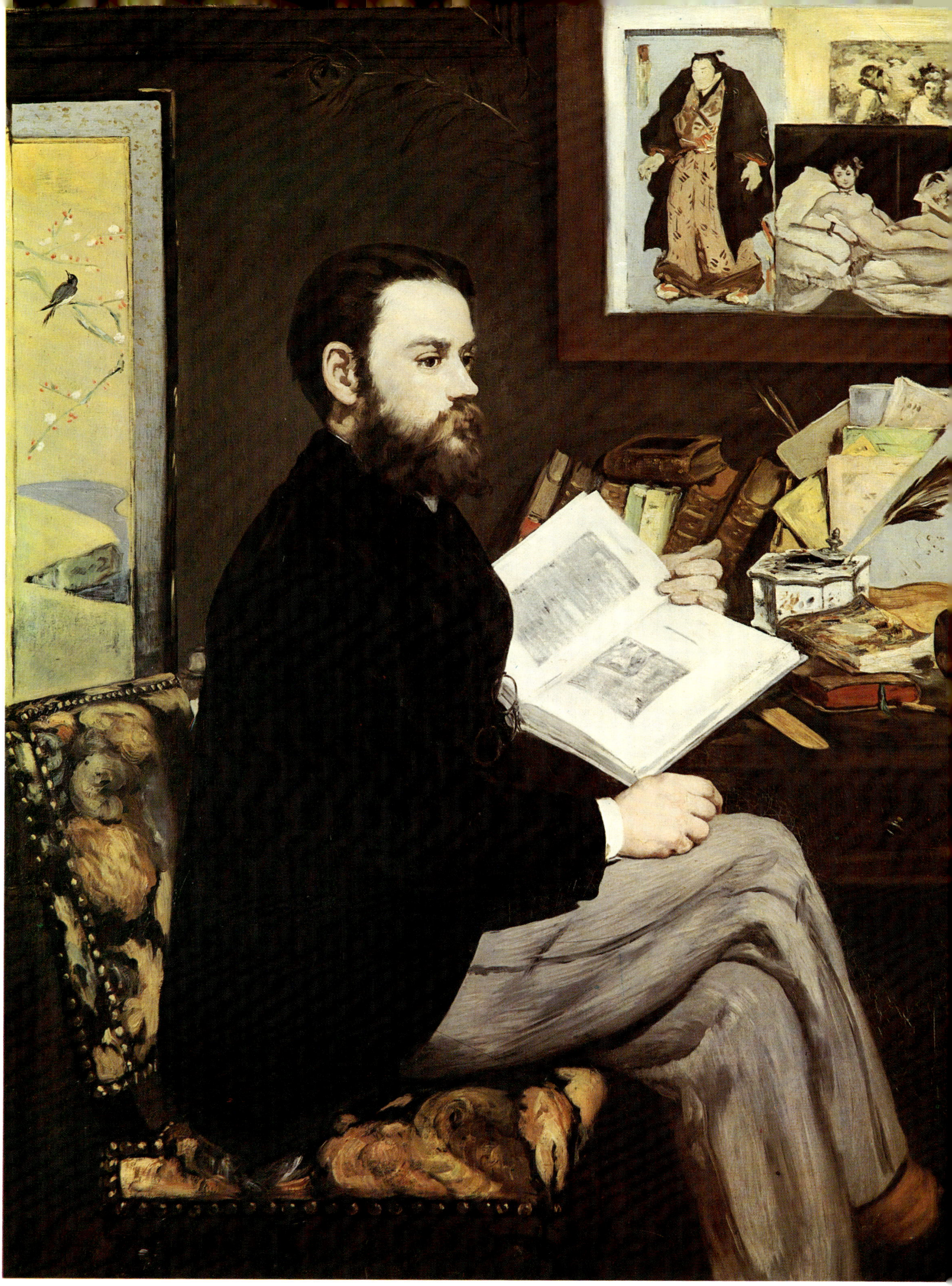

17. *Portrait of Emile Zola* - 1868. Musée d'Orsay, Paris

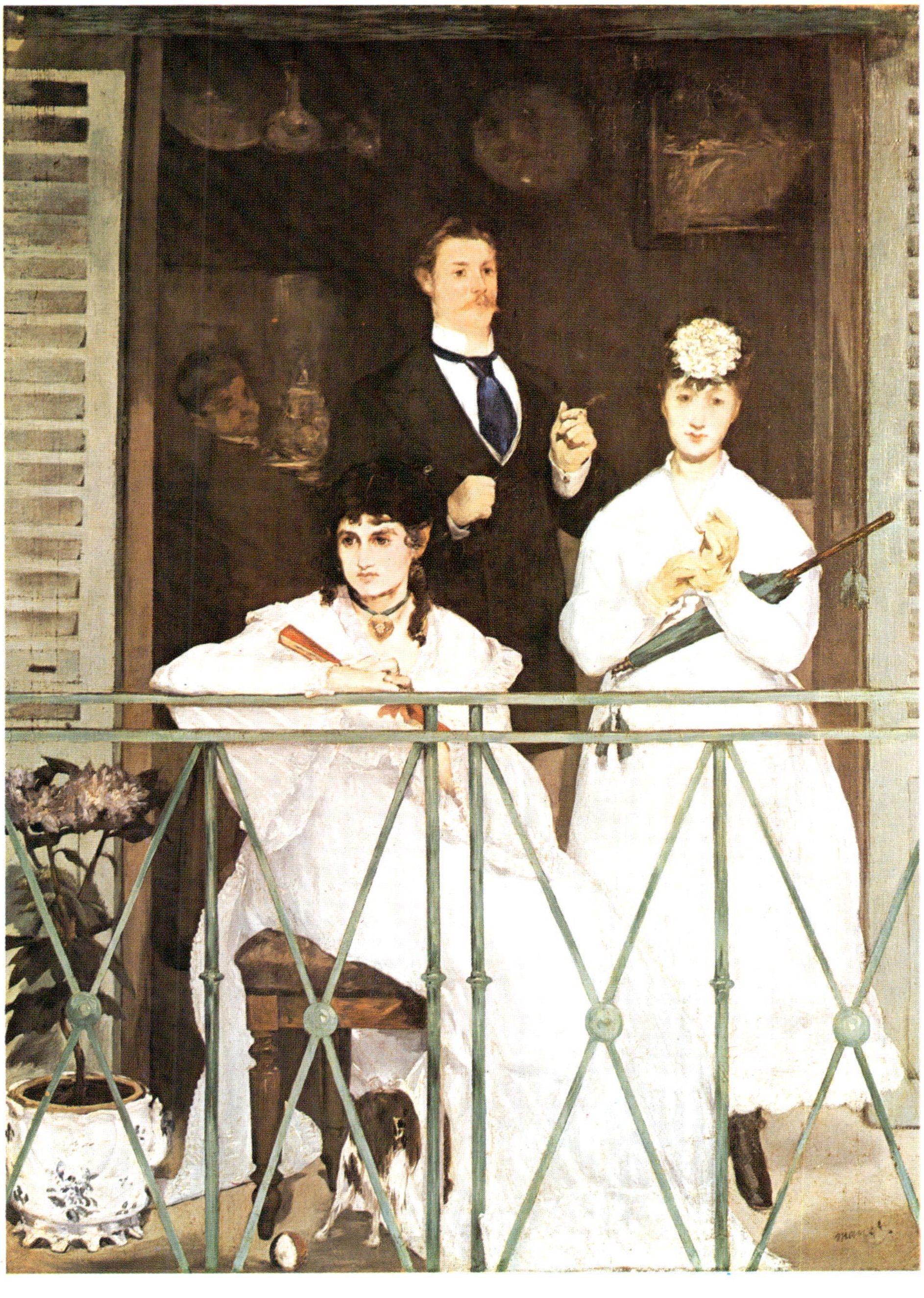

18. *The Balcony* - 1868-69. Musée d'Orsay, Paris

19. *Portrait of Guillaudin on Horseback* - 1870. Private collection, Michigan

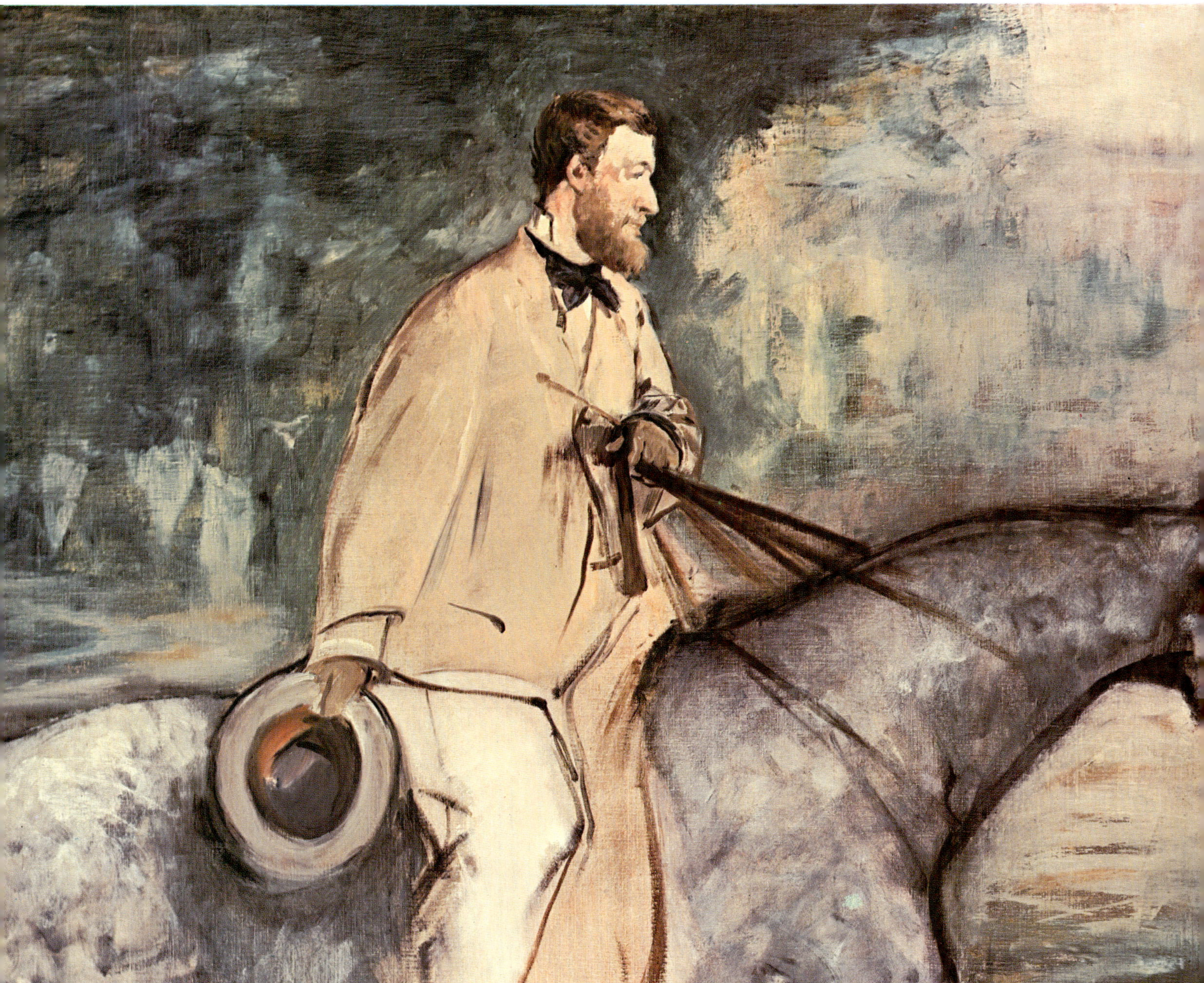

20. *The Greyhound* - 1871. Private collection

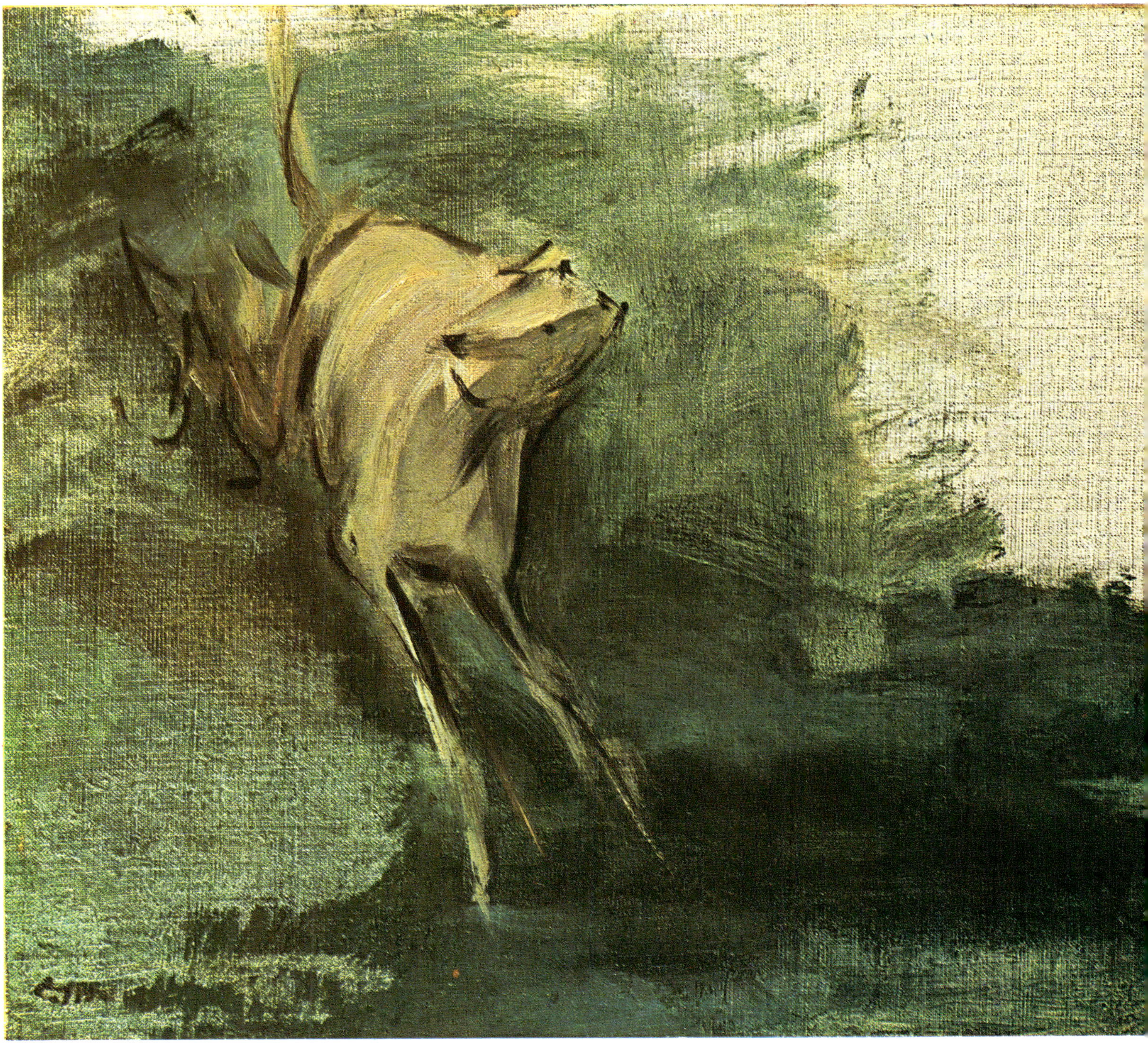

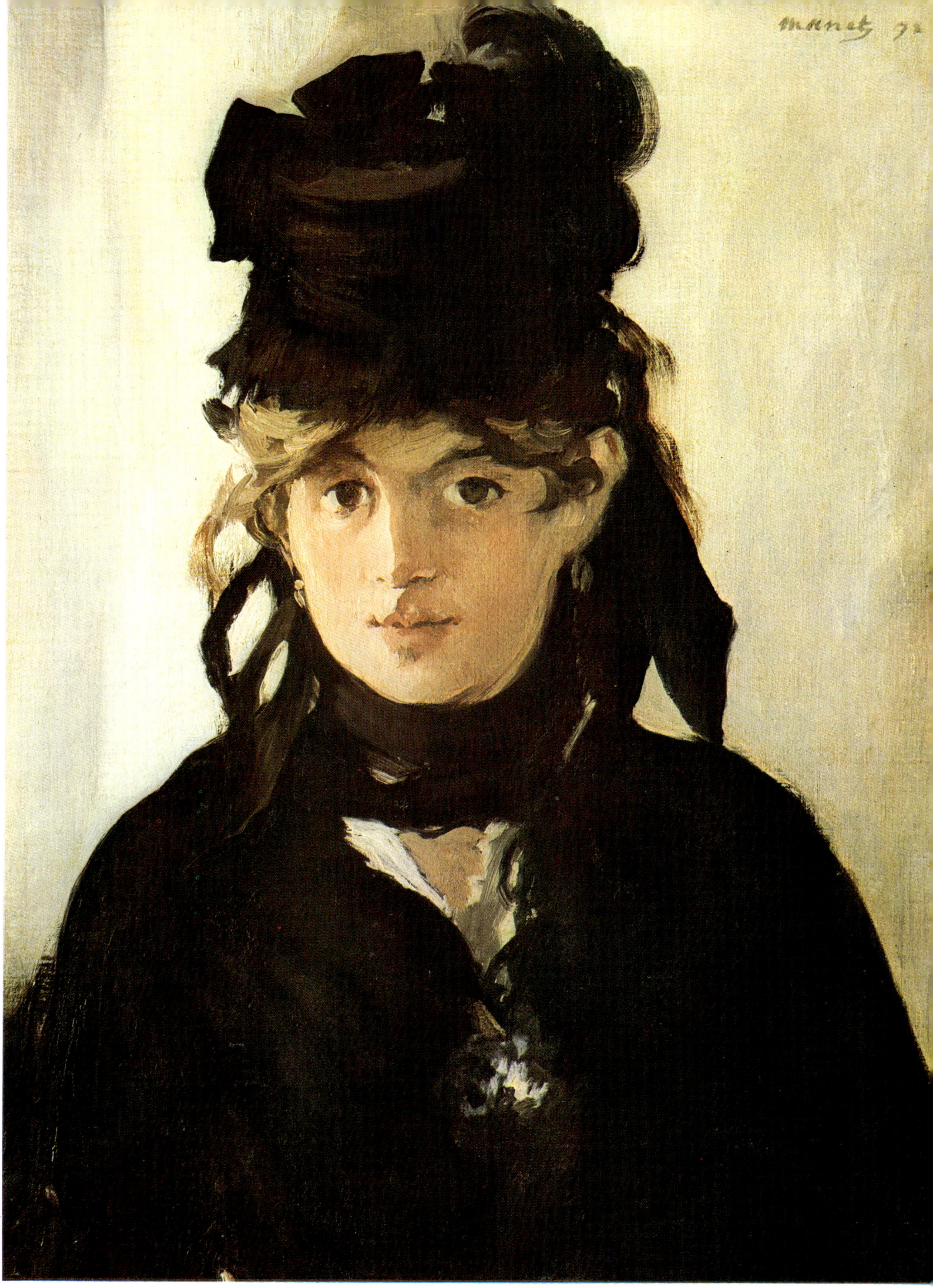
manet 72

21. *Berthe Morisot with a Bunch of Violets* - 1872. Private collection, Paris

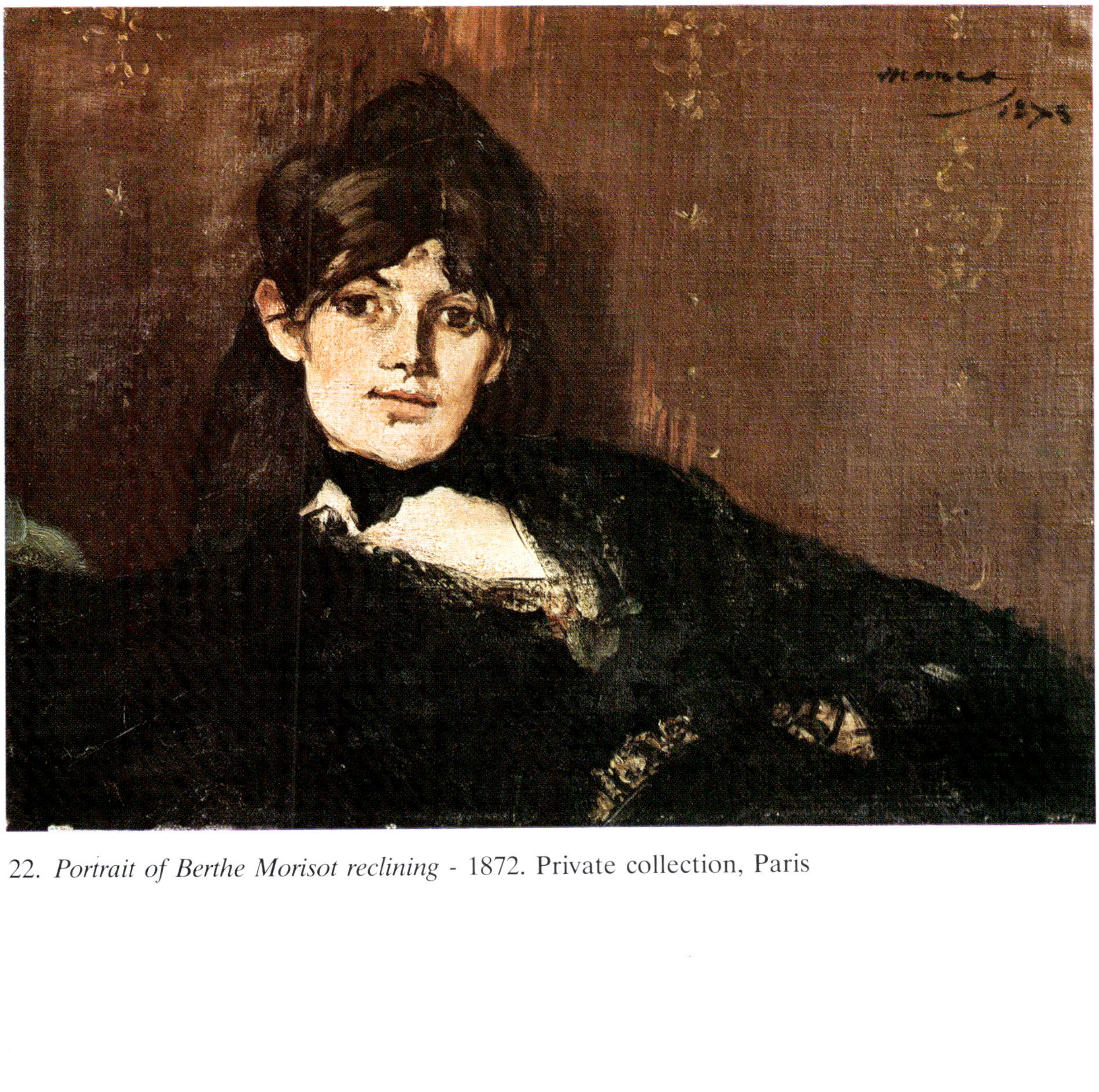

22. *Portrait of Berthe Morisot reclining* - 1872. Private collection, Paris

23. *Lunch in the Studio* - 1868.
Bayerische Staatsgemälde Sammlungen, Munich

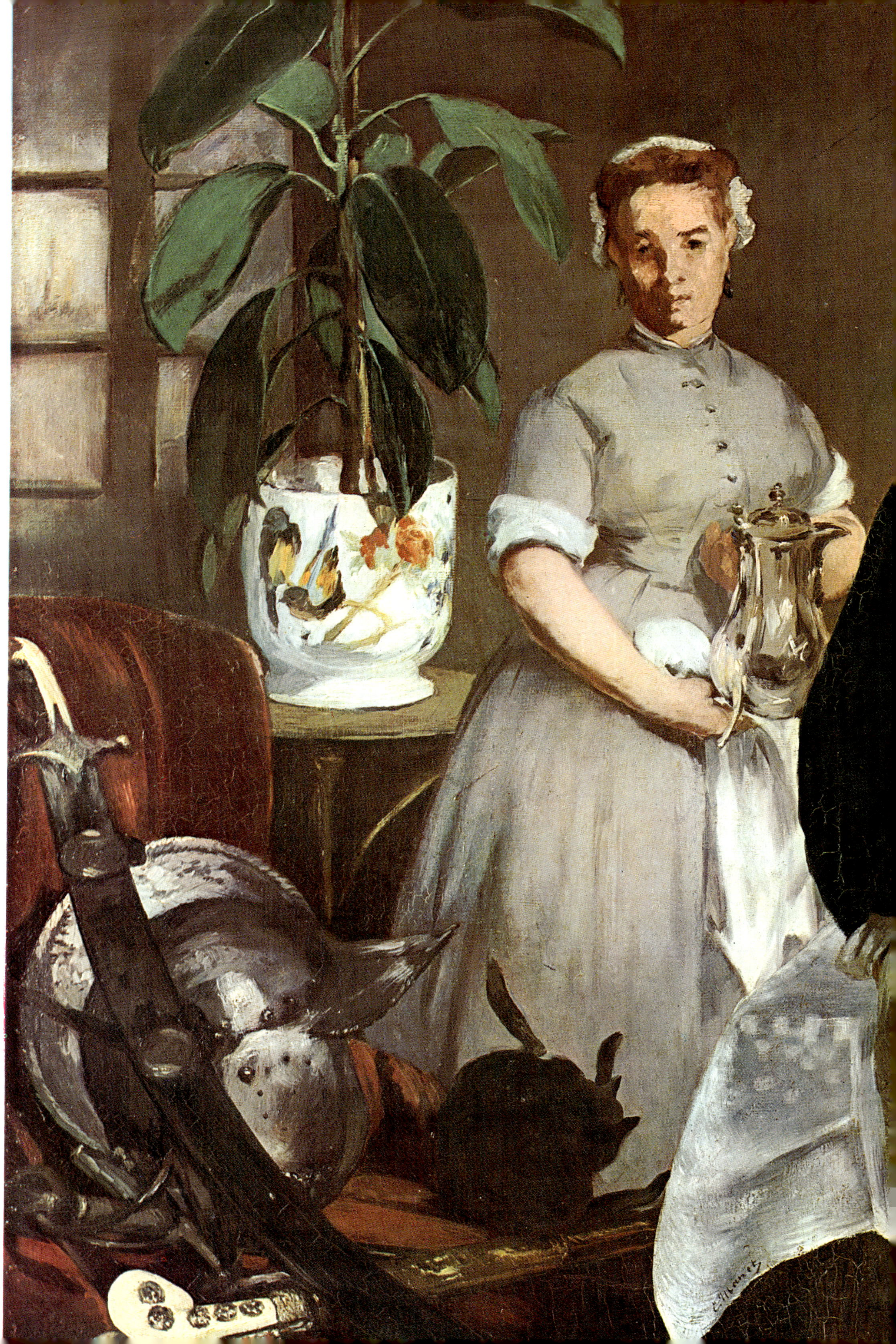
E. Manet

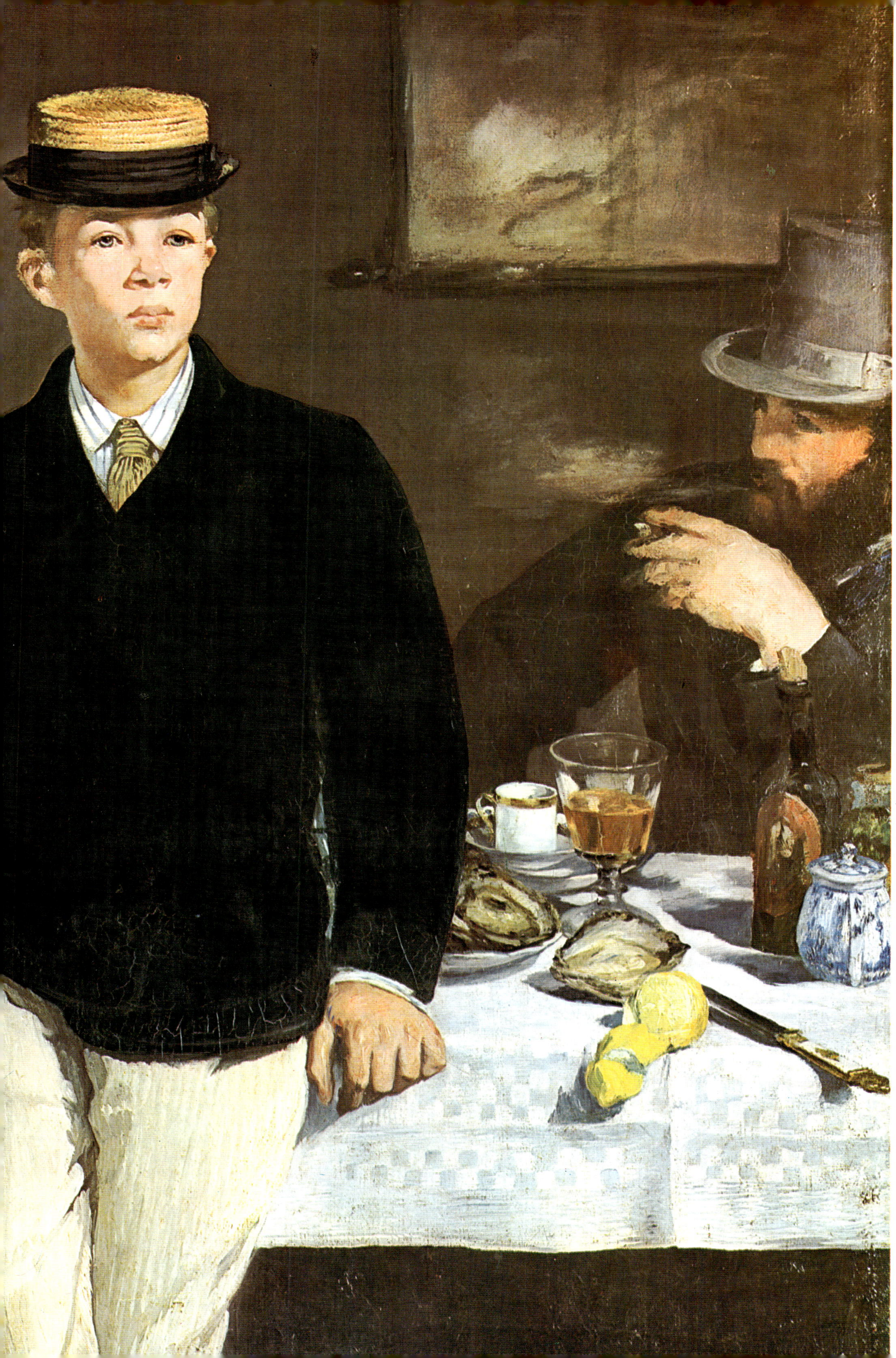

24. *On the Beach at Boulogne* - 1873. Musée d'Orsay, Paris

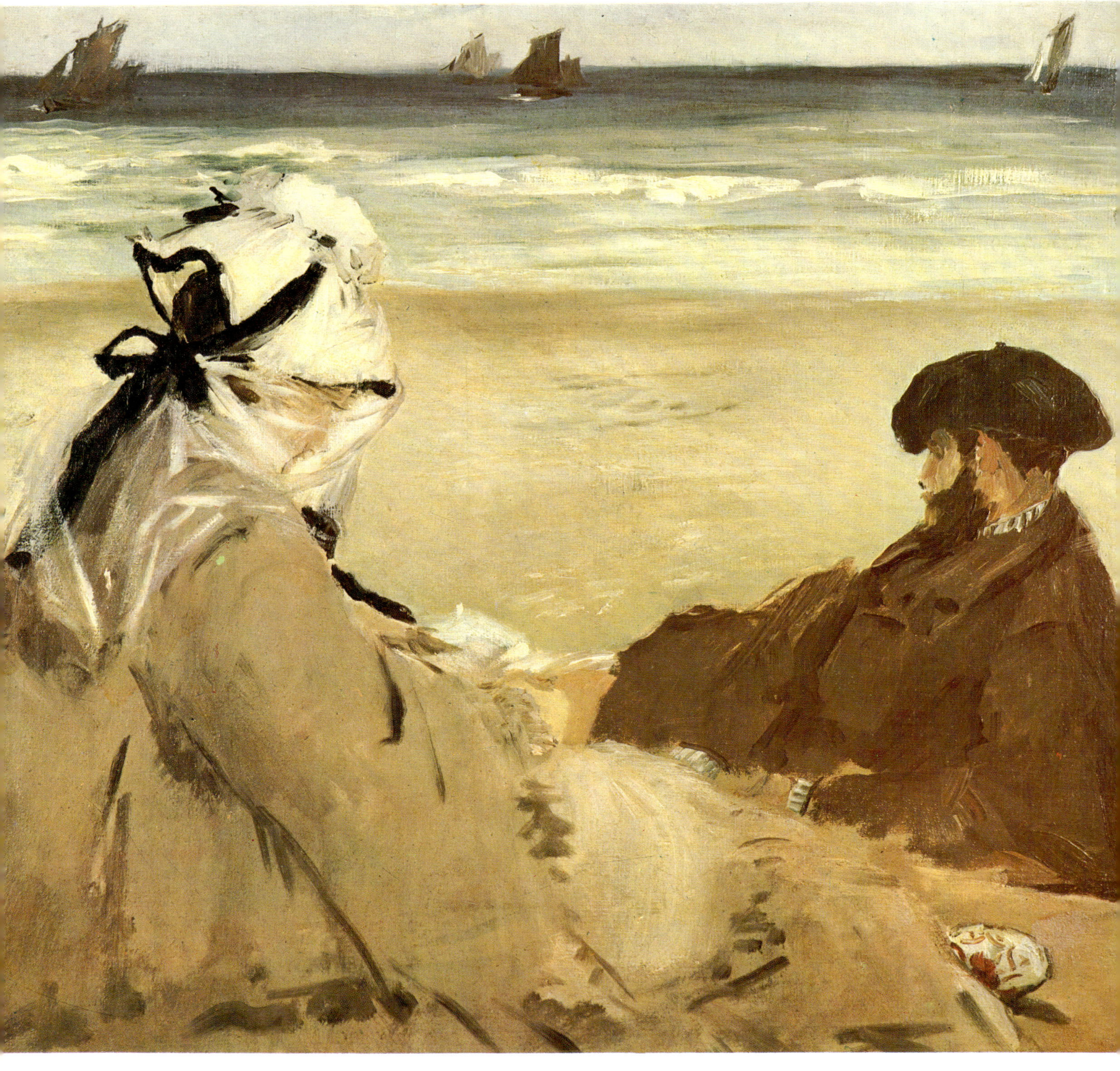

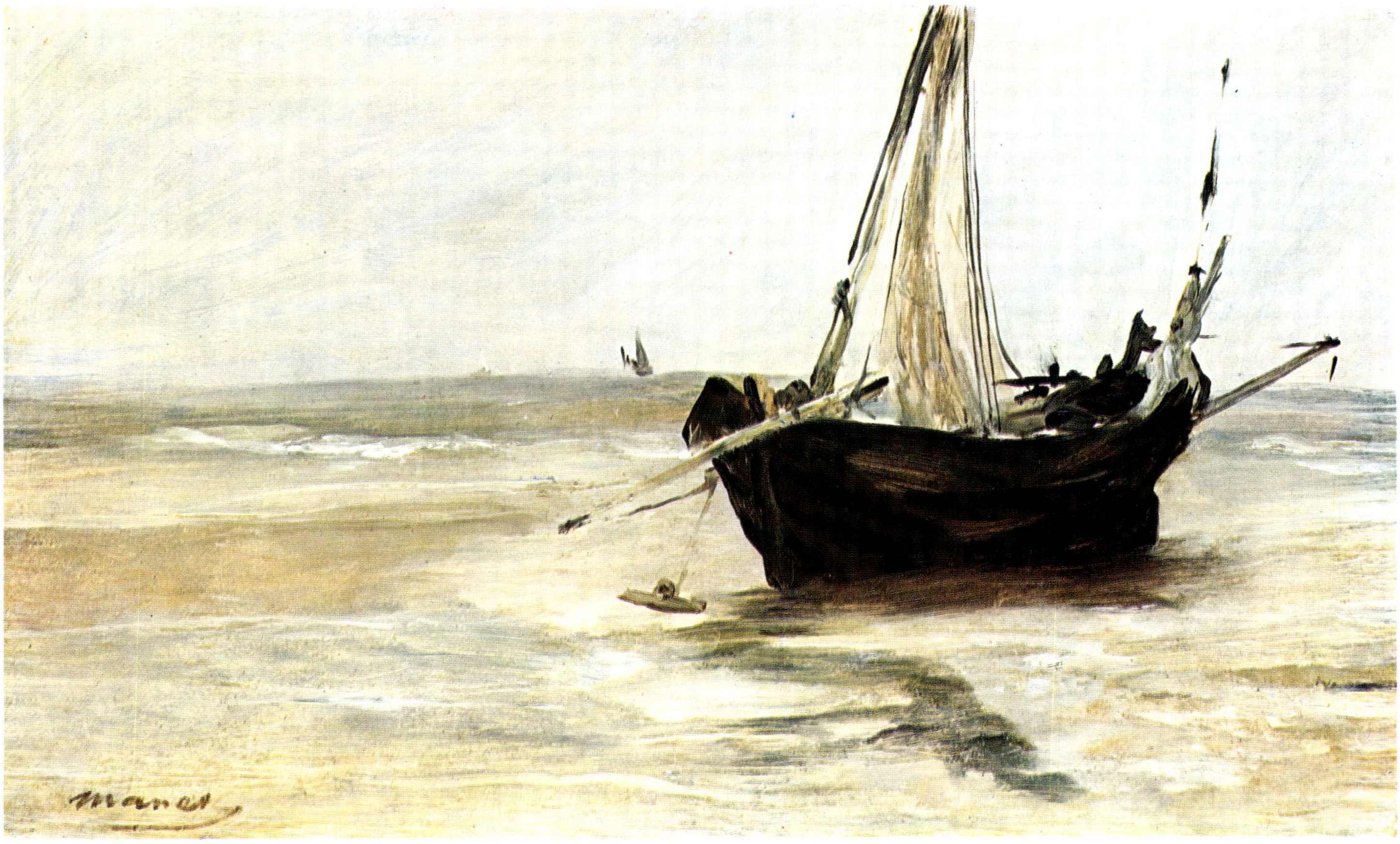

25. *The Black Boat at Berck* - 1873. Private collection

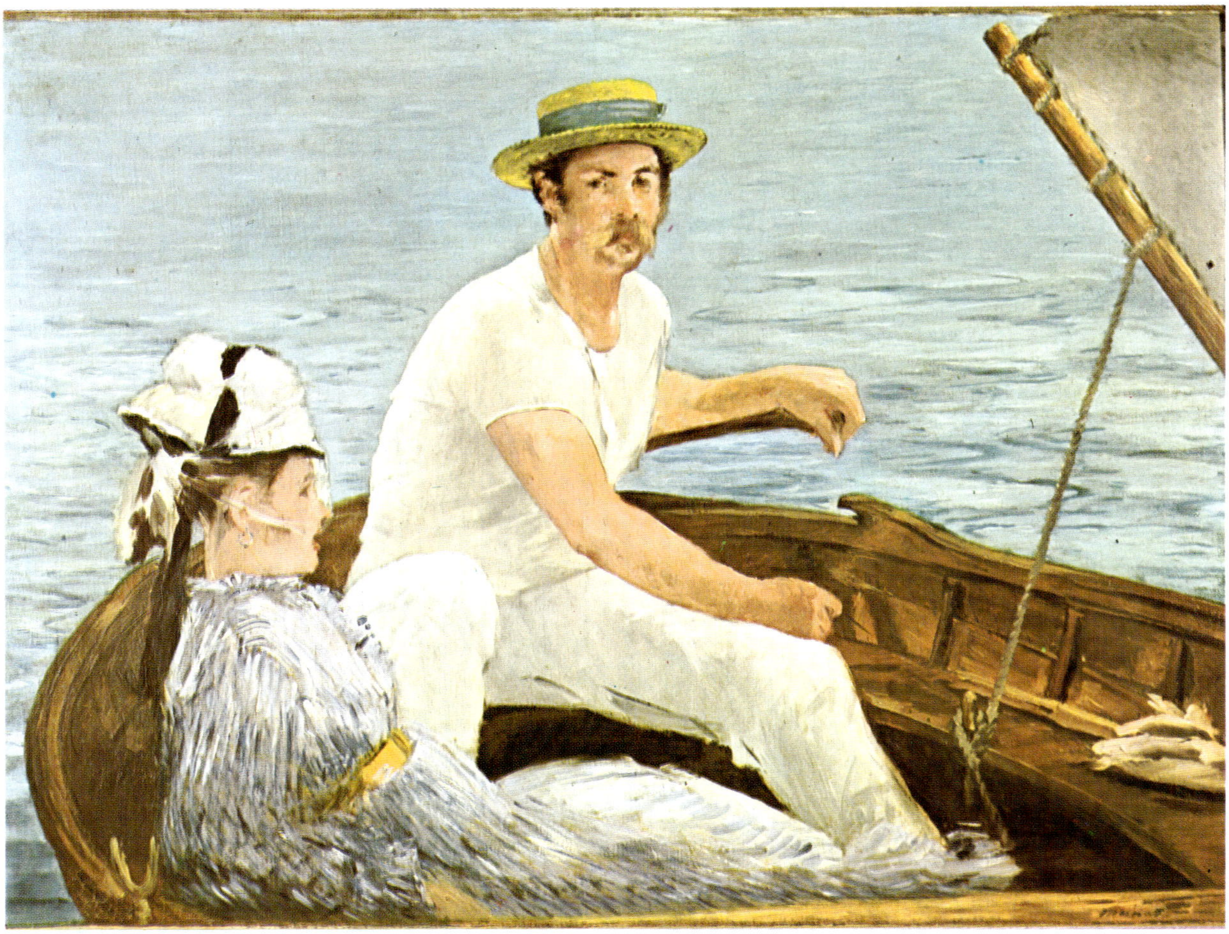

26. *The Boat* - 1874. Metropolitan Museum of Art, New York

27. *Monet in his Studio Boat* - 1874. Neue Pinakothek, Munich

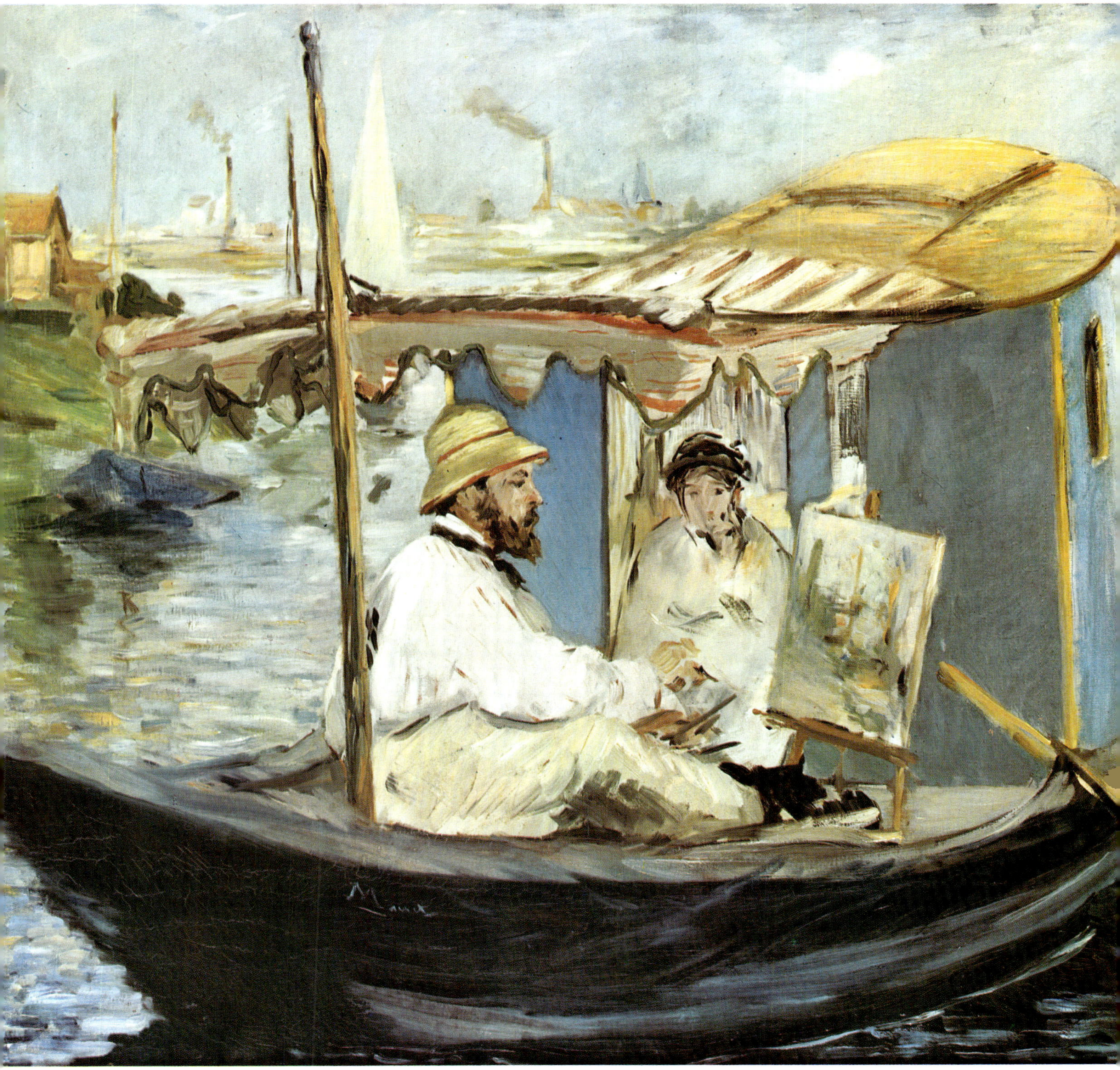

28. *Portrait of Stéphane Mallarmé* - 1876. Musée du Louvre, Paris

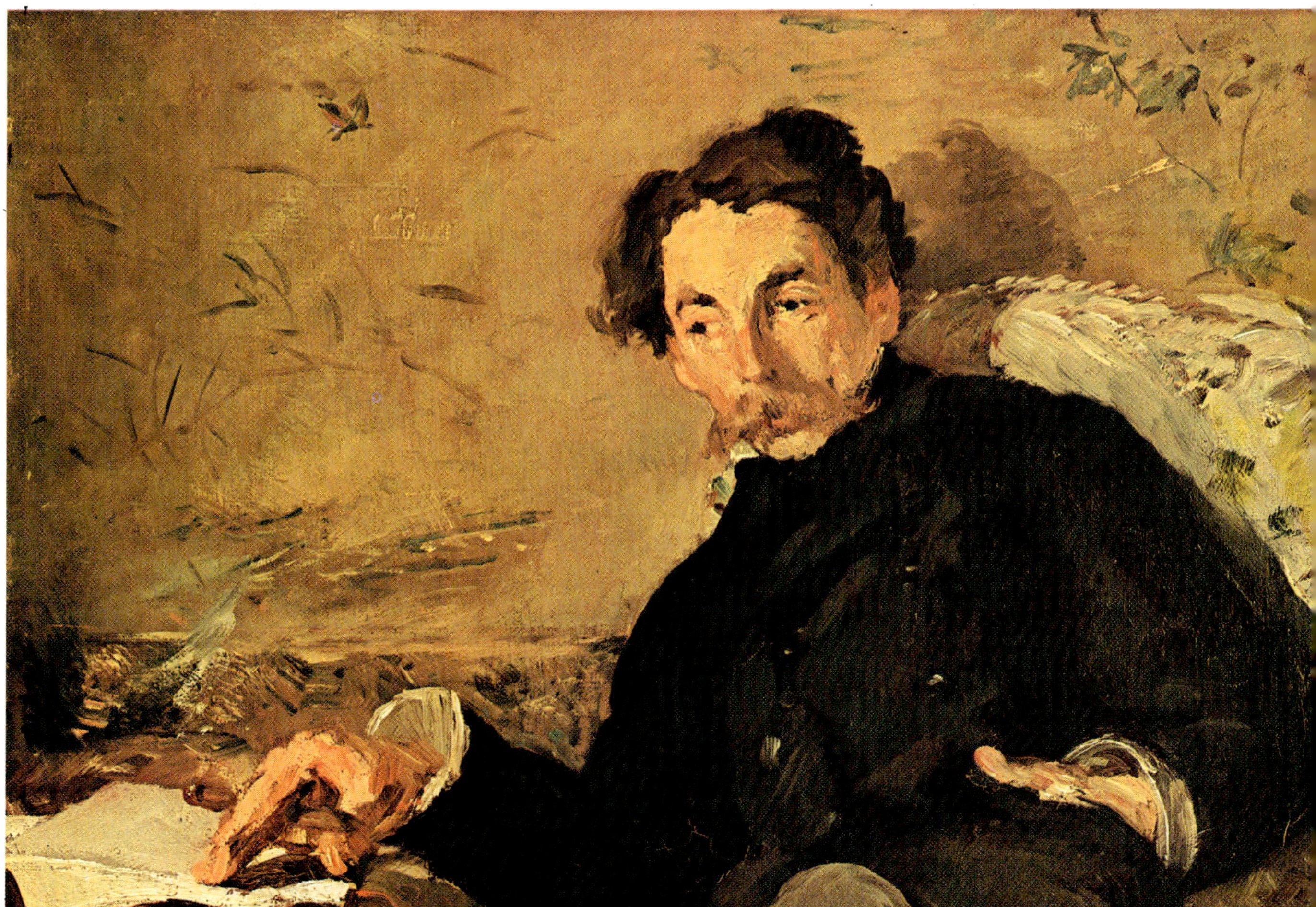

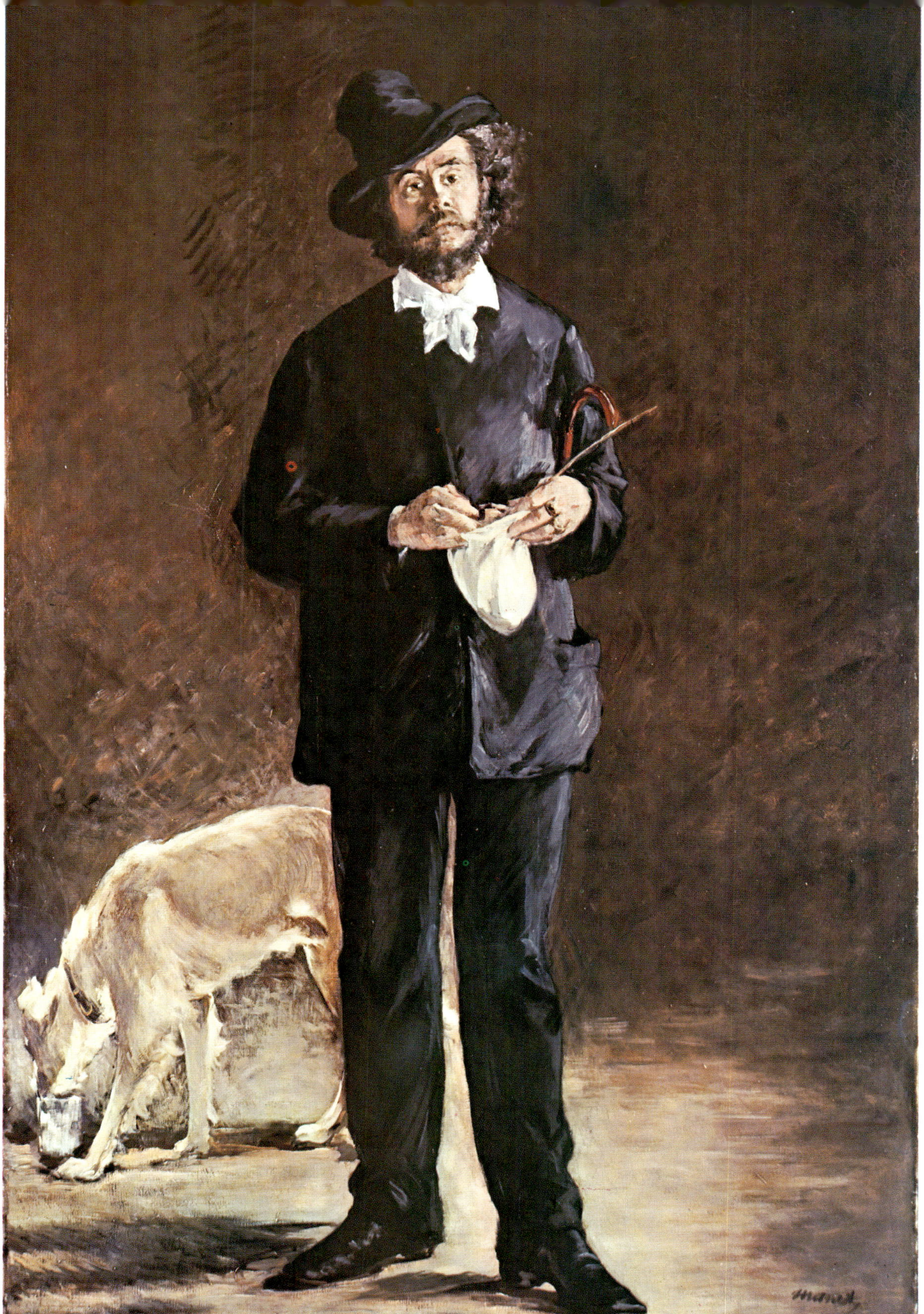

29. *The Artist* - 1875. Museu de Arte, São Paulo

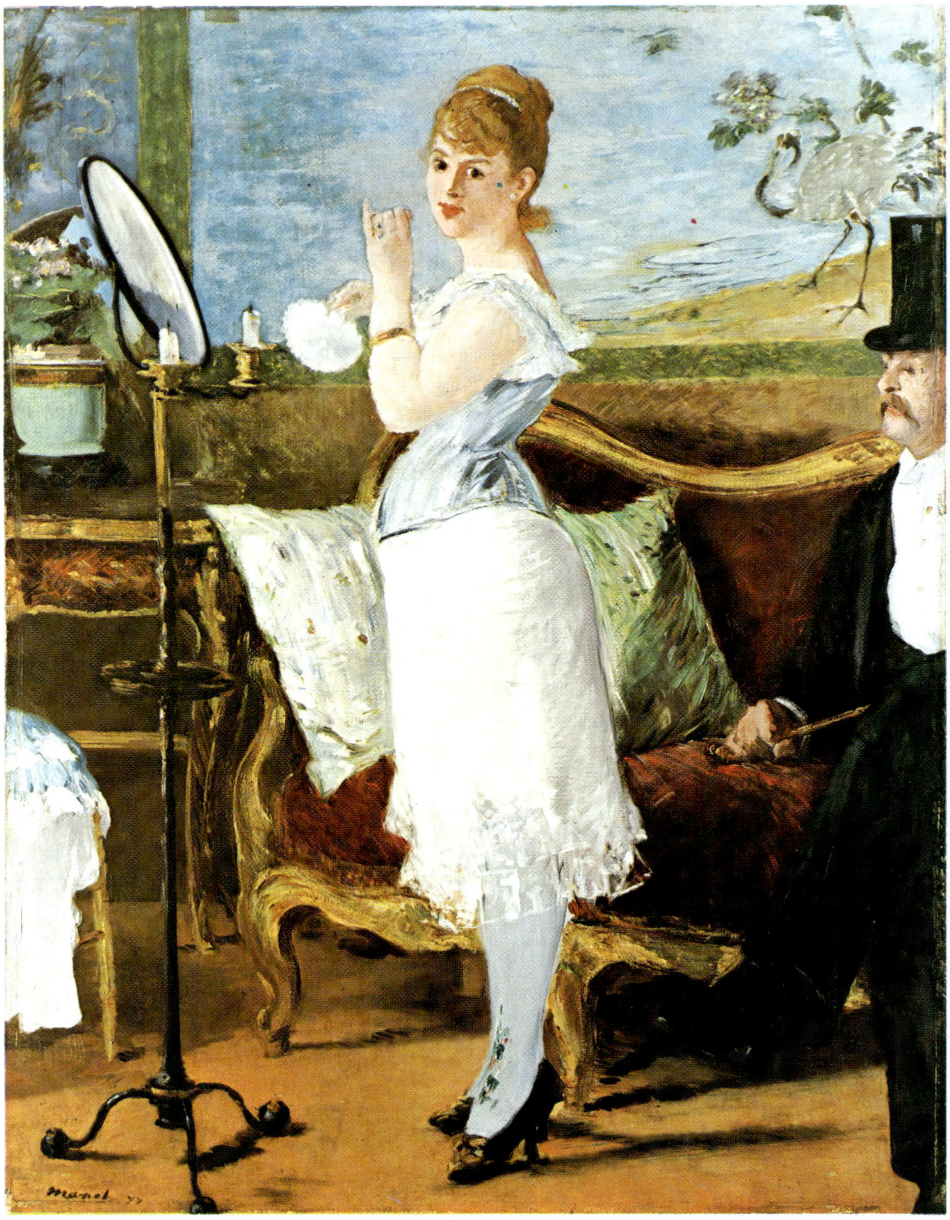

30. *Nana* - 1877. Kunsthalle, Hamburg

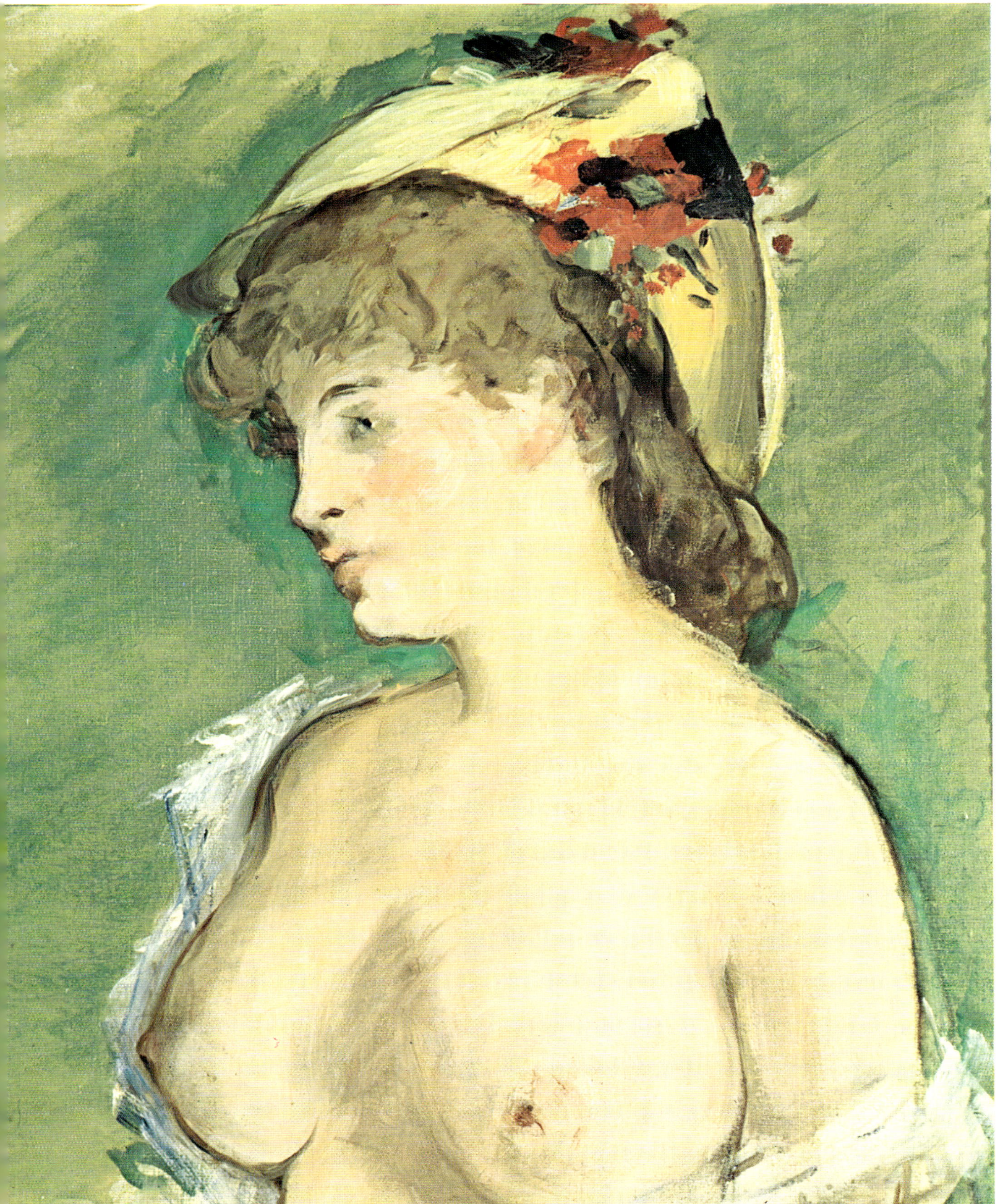

31. *Blonde Semi-nude* - 1875. Musée du Louvre, Paris

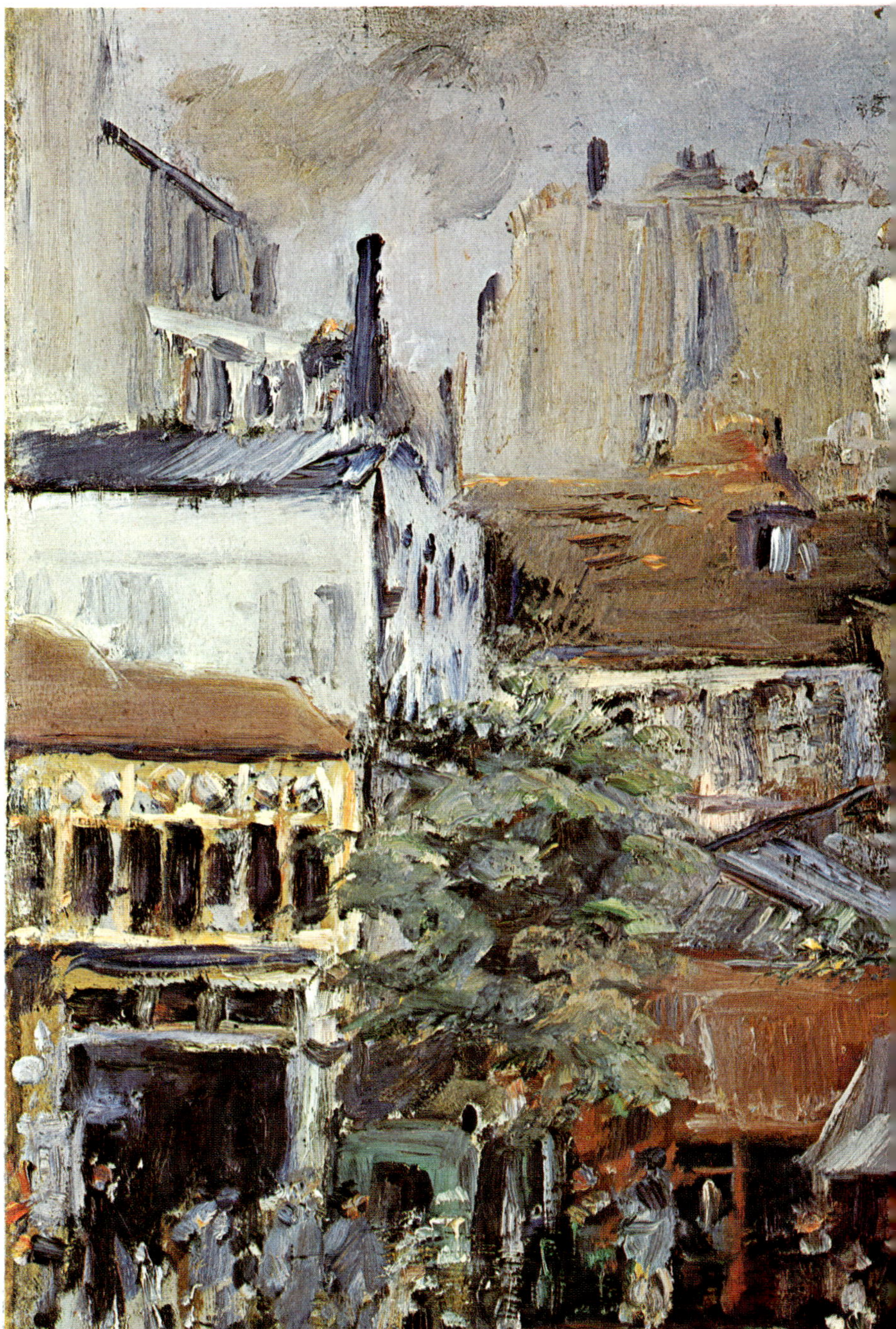

32. *View from near the Place Clichy* - 1875-78. Private collection

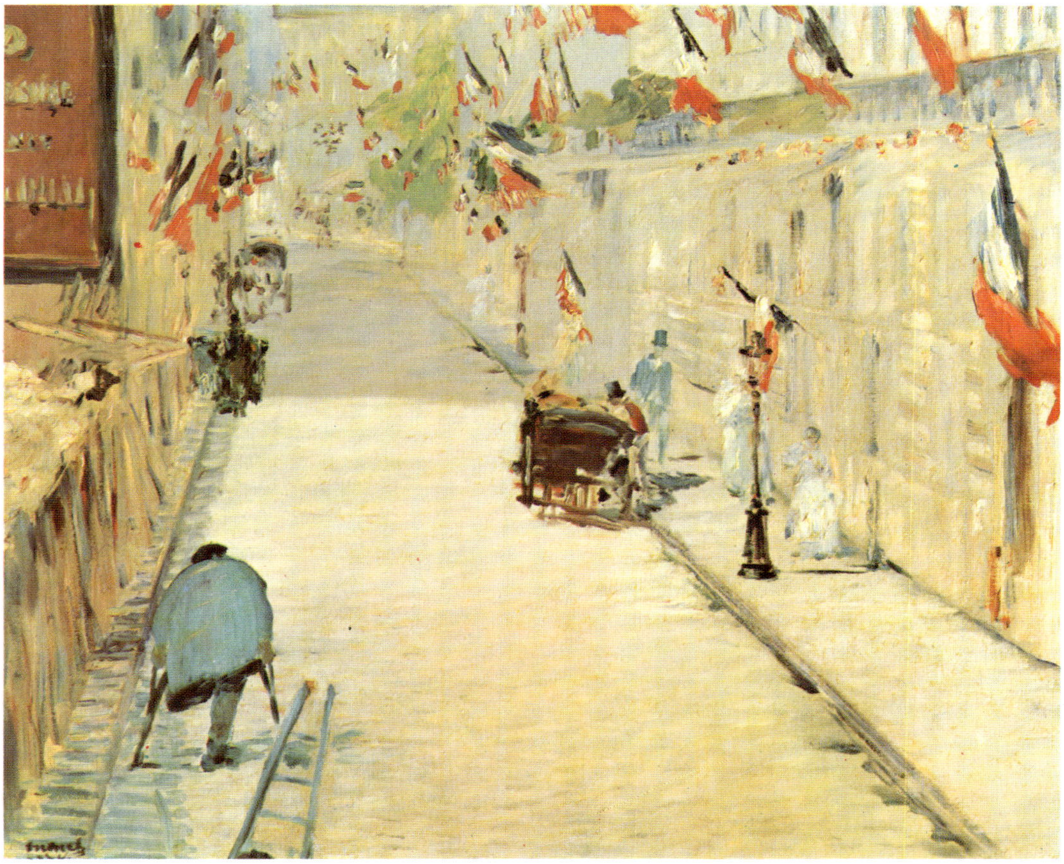

33. *Rue Mosnier Decked with Flags* - 1878. Private collection, Virginia

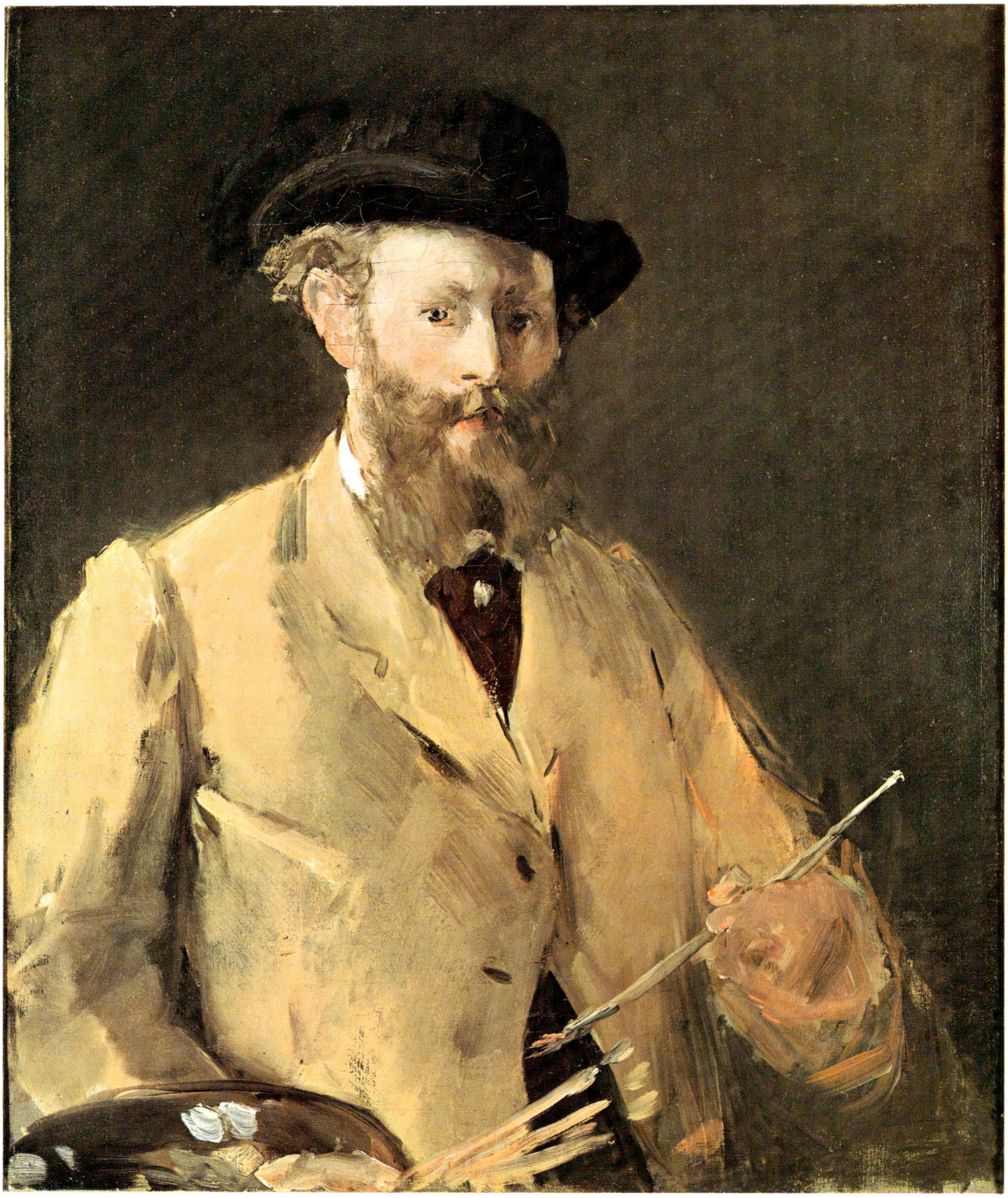

34. *Self-Portrait* - 1879. Private collection, New York

35. *At the Café* - 1878. O. Reinhart am Roemerholz Collection, Winterthur

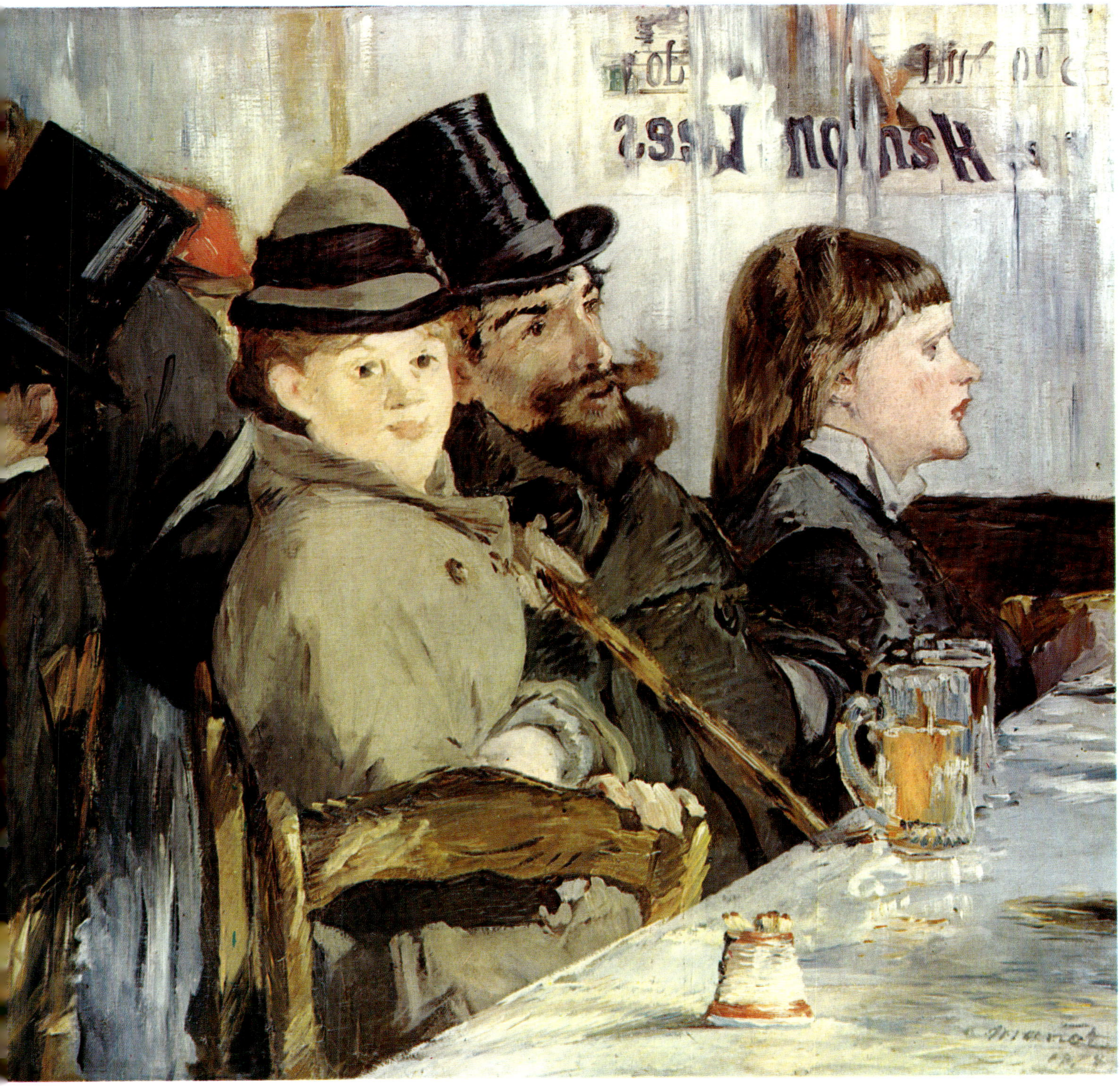

36. *Isabelle Lemonnier, seated* - 1878-79. Private collection

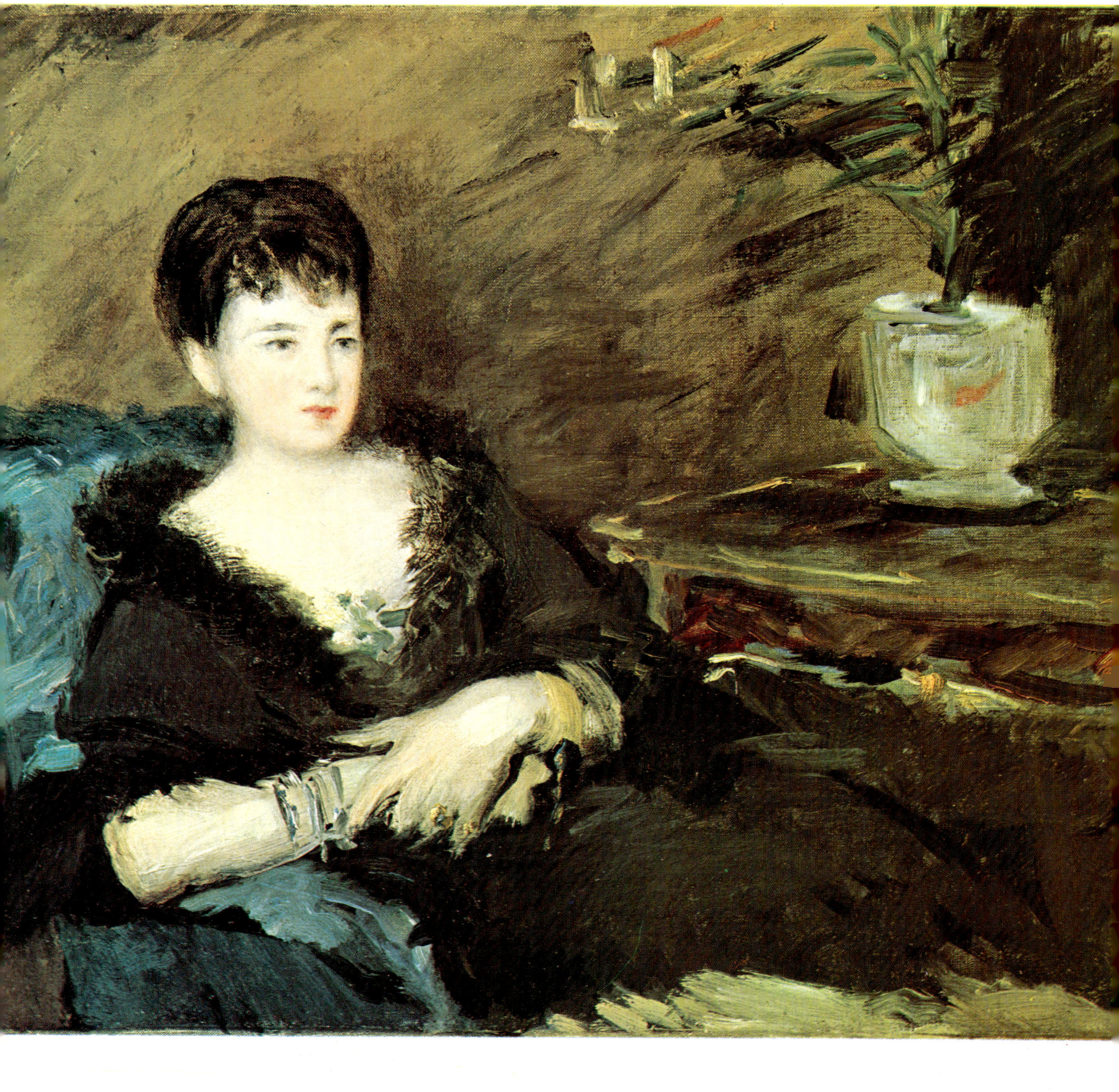

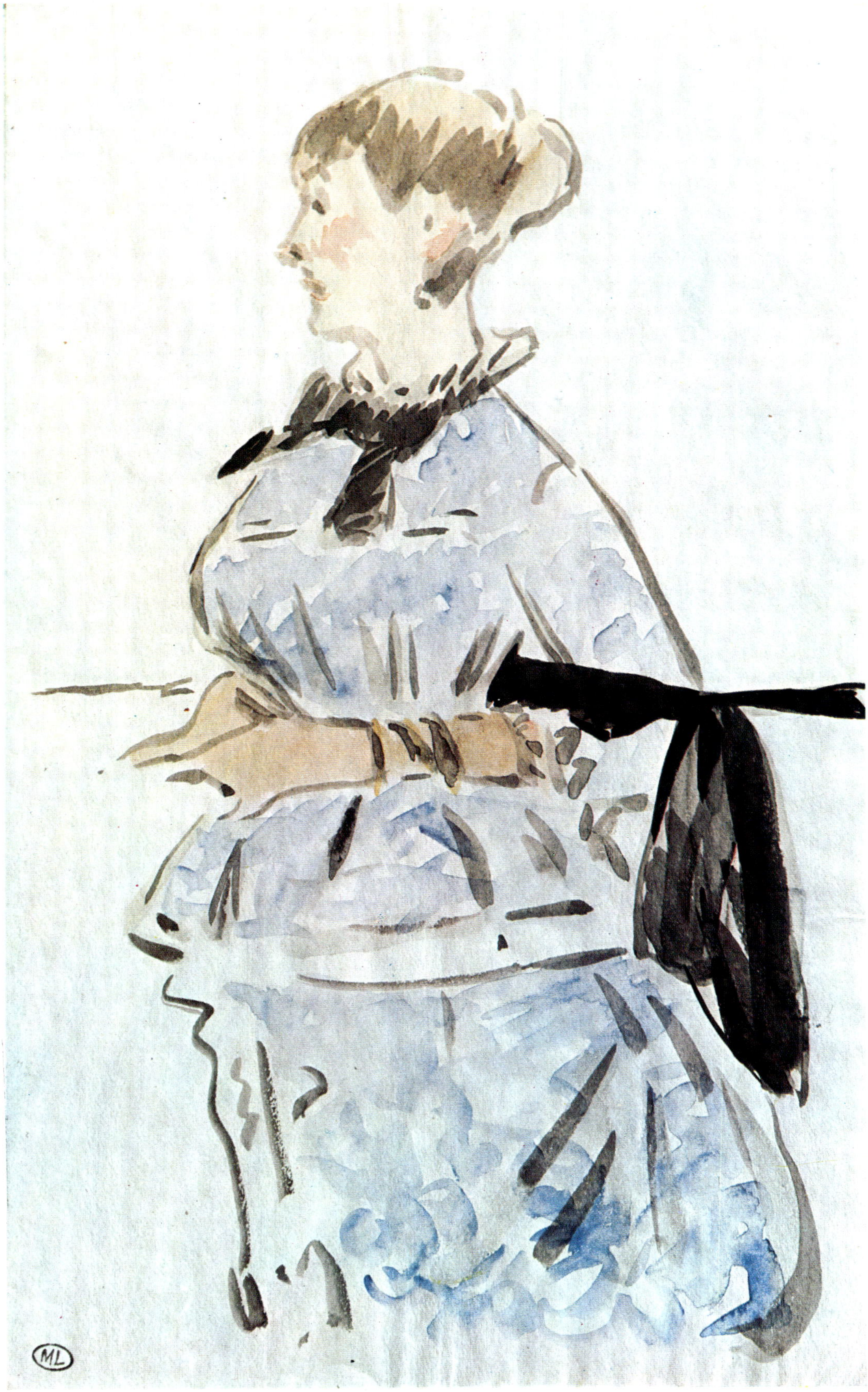

37. *Isabelle Lemonnier* - 1880. Musée du Louvre, Paris

38. *The Café on the rue du Théâtre Français* - date unknown. Burrell Collection, Glasgow

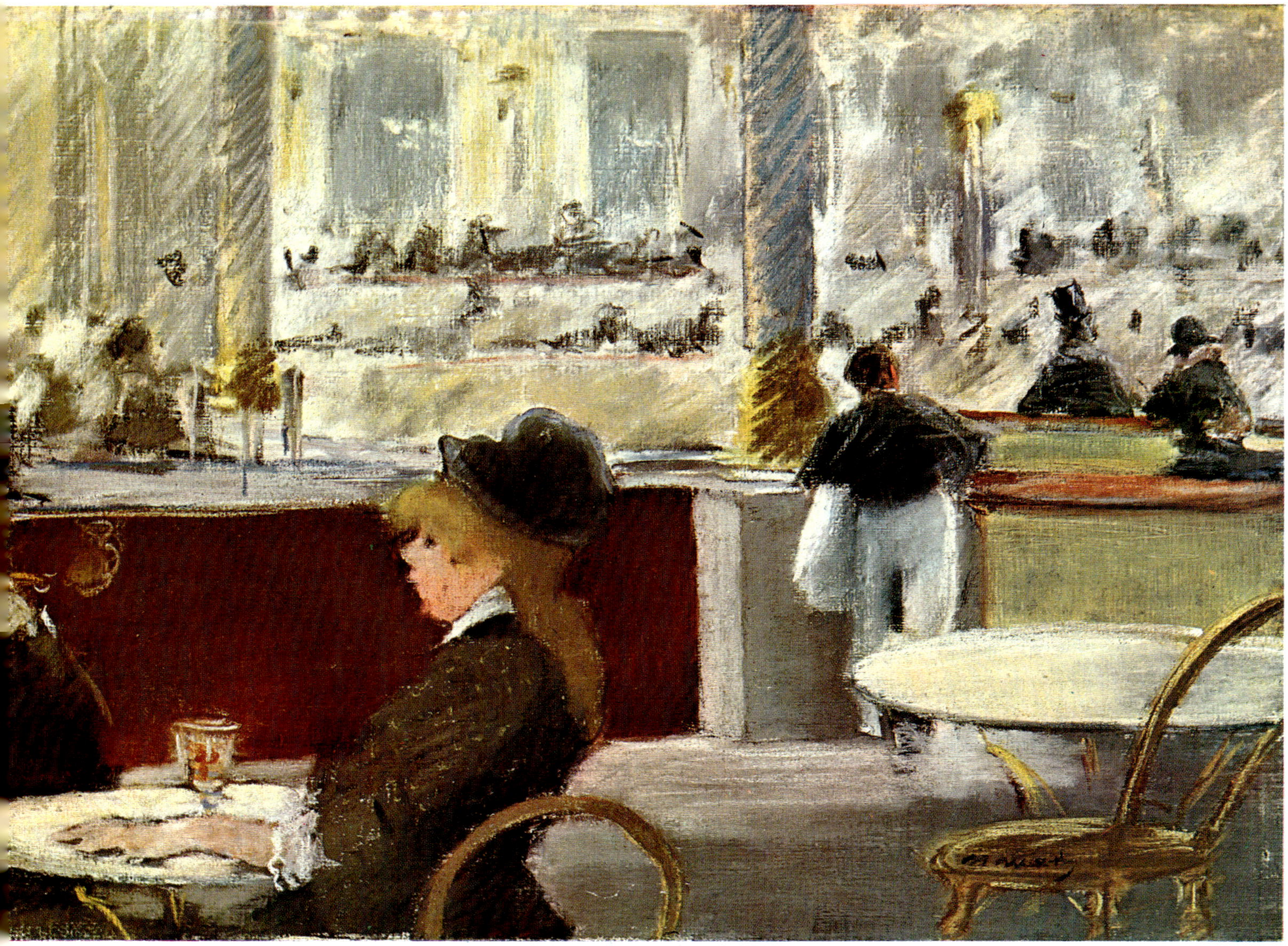

39. *The Bon Bock* - 1879. Musée d'Orsay, Paris

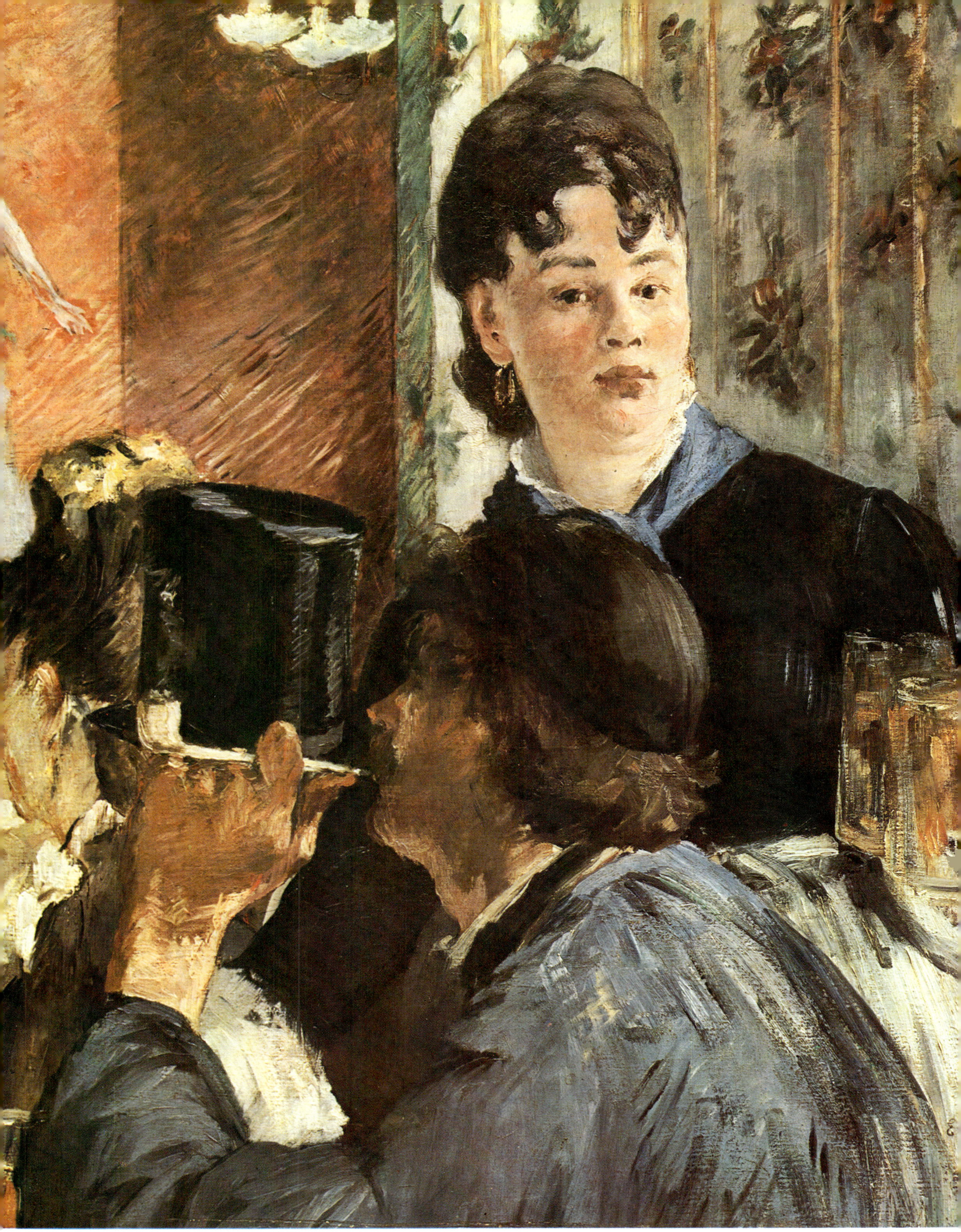

40. *Manet's Mother in the Garden of Bellevue* - 1880. Private collection, Paris

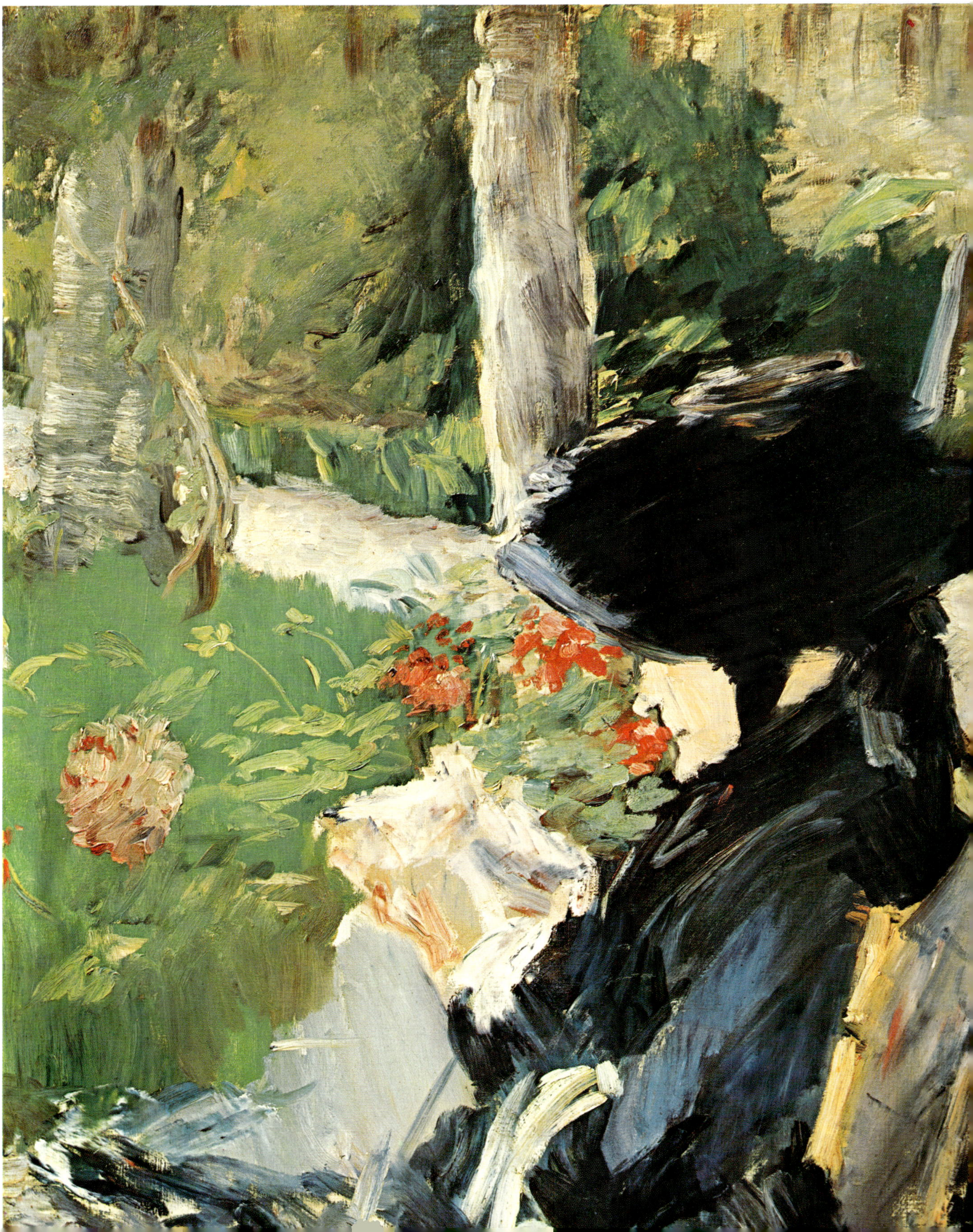

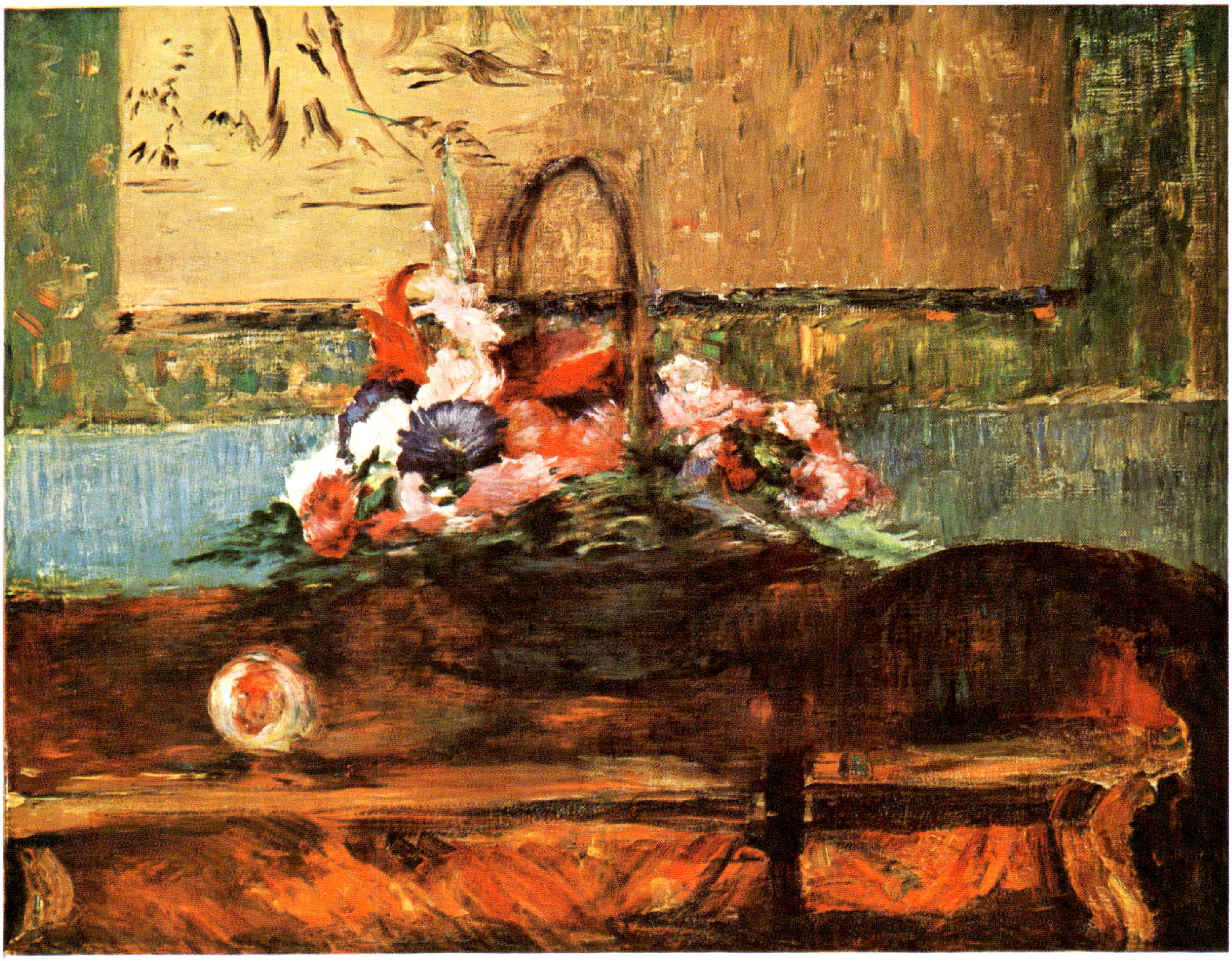

41. *Basket of Flowers* - 1880. Private collection

42. *Spring (Jeanne de Marsy)* - 1881. Private collection, New York

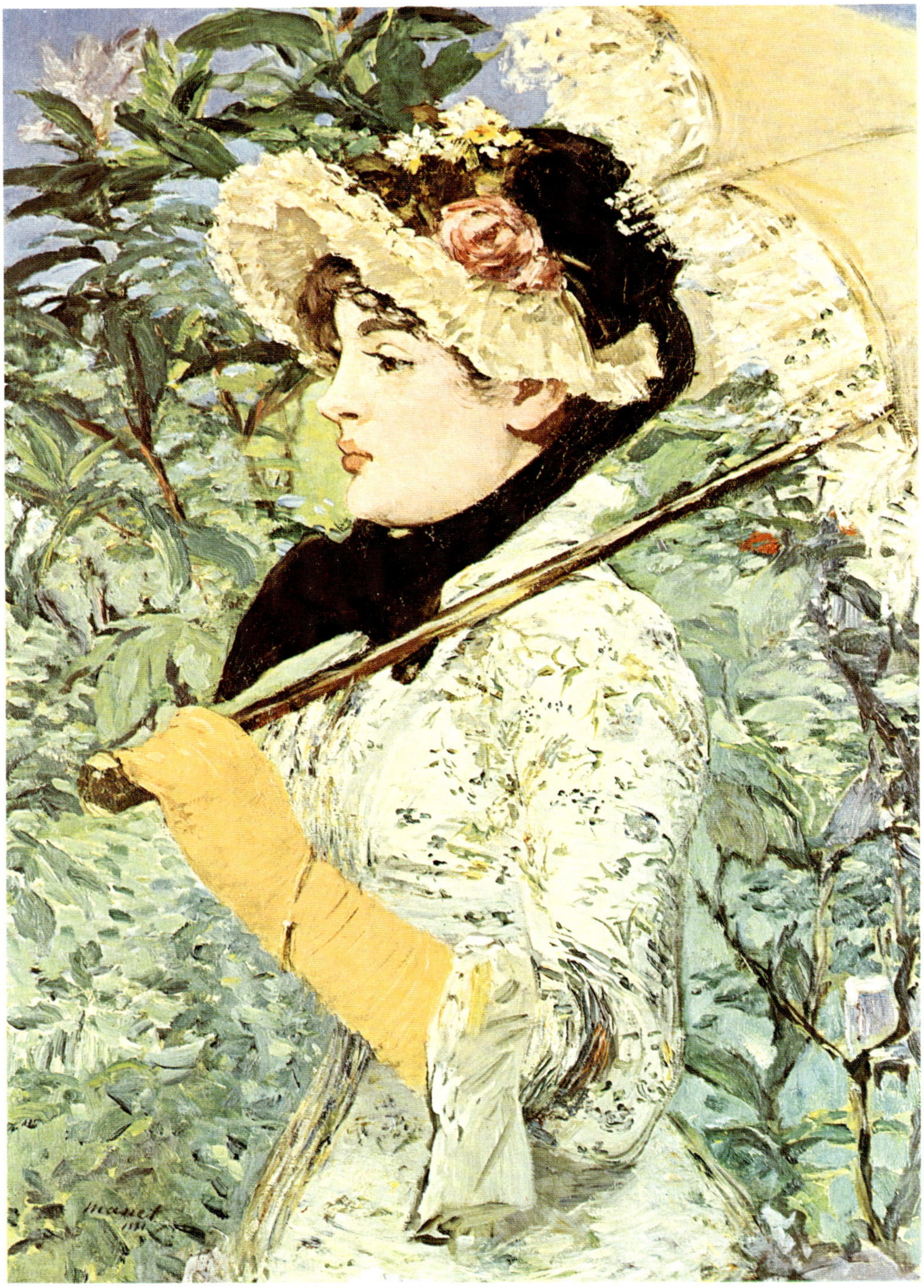

43. *Model for Bar at the Folies-Bergère* - 1881.
Musée des Beaux-Arts, Dijon

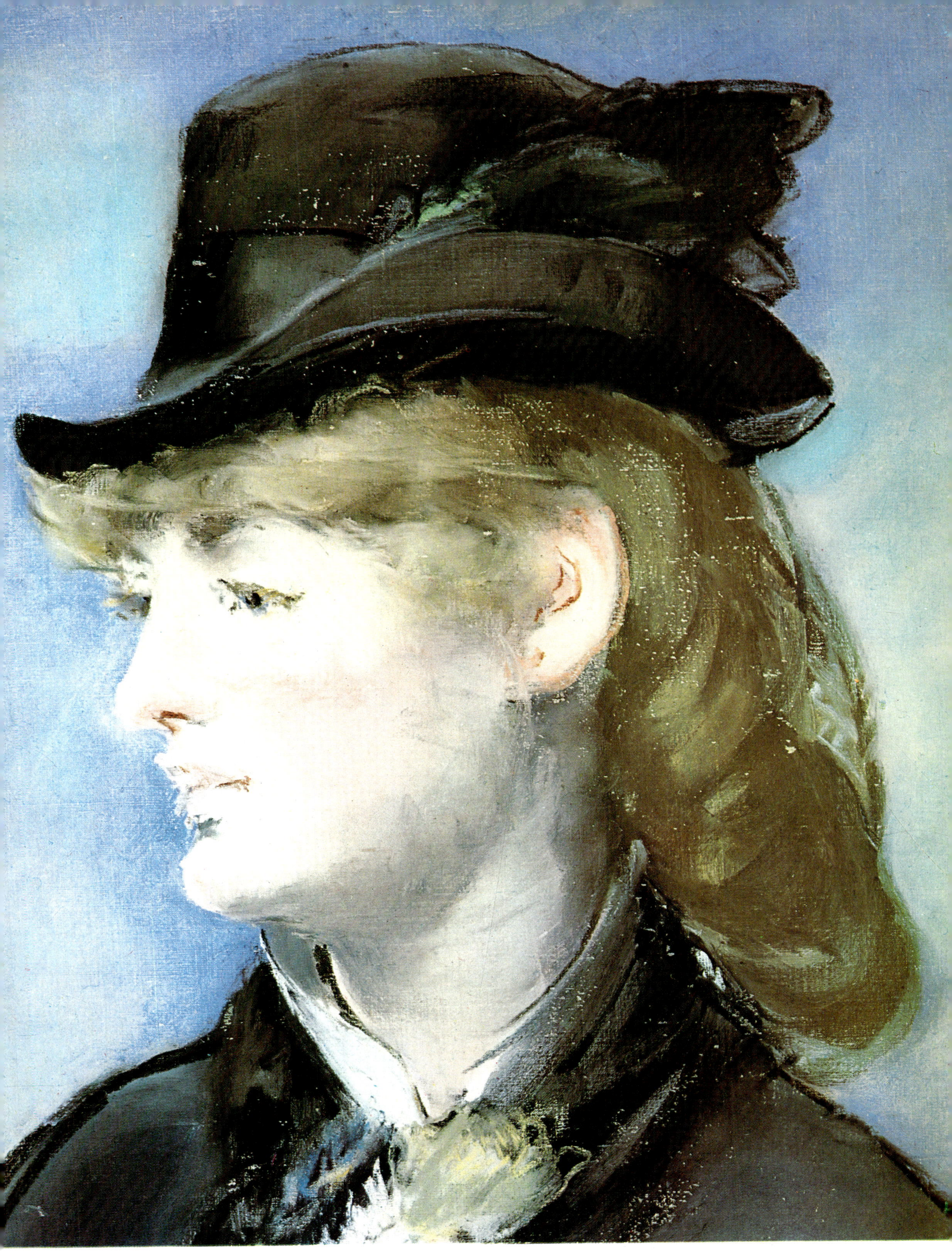

44. *Bar at the Folies-Bergère* - 1881-82. Courtauld Institute Galleries, London

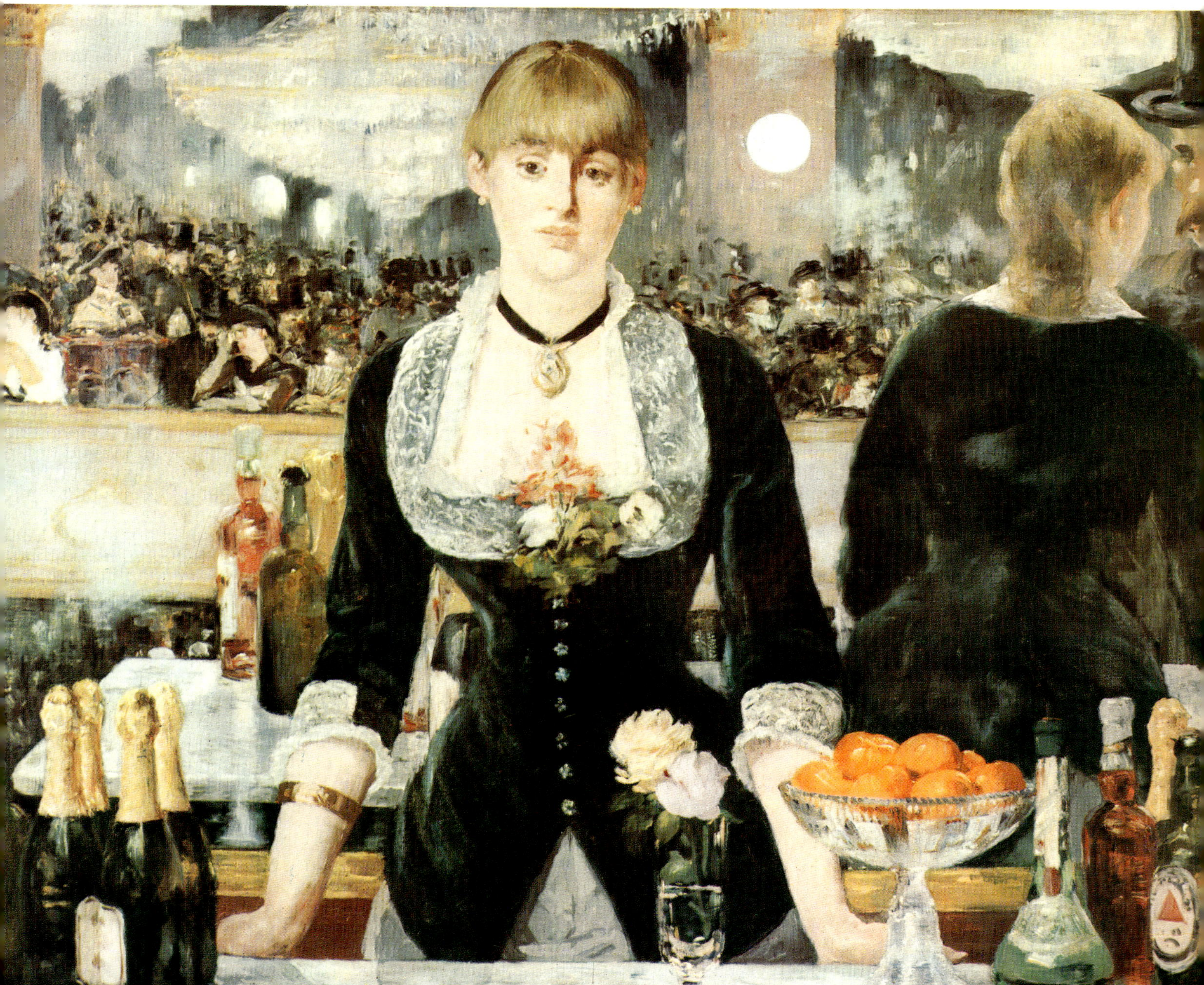

45. *Autumn (Méry Laurent)* - 1881-82. Musée des Beaux-Arts, Nancy

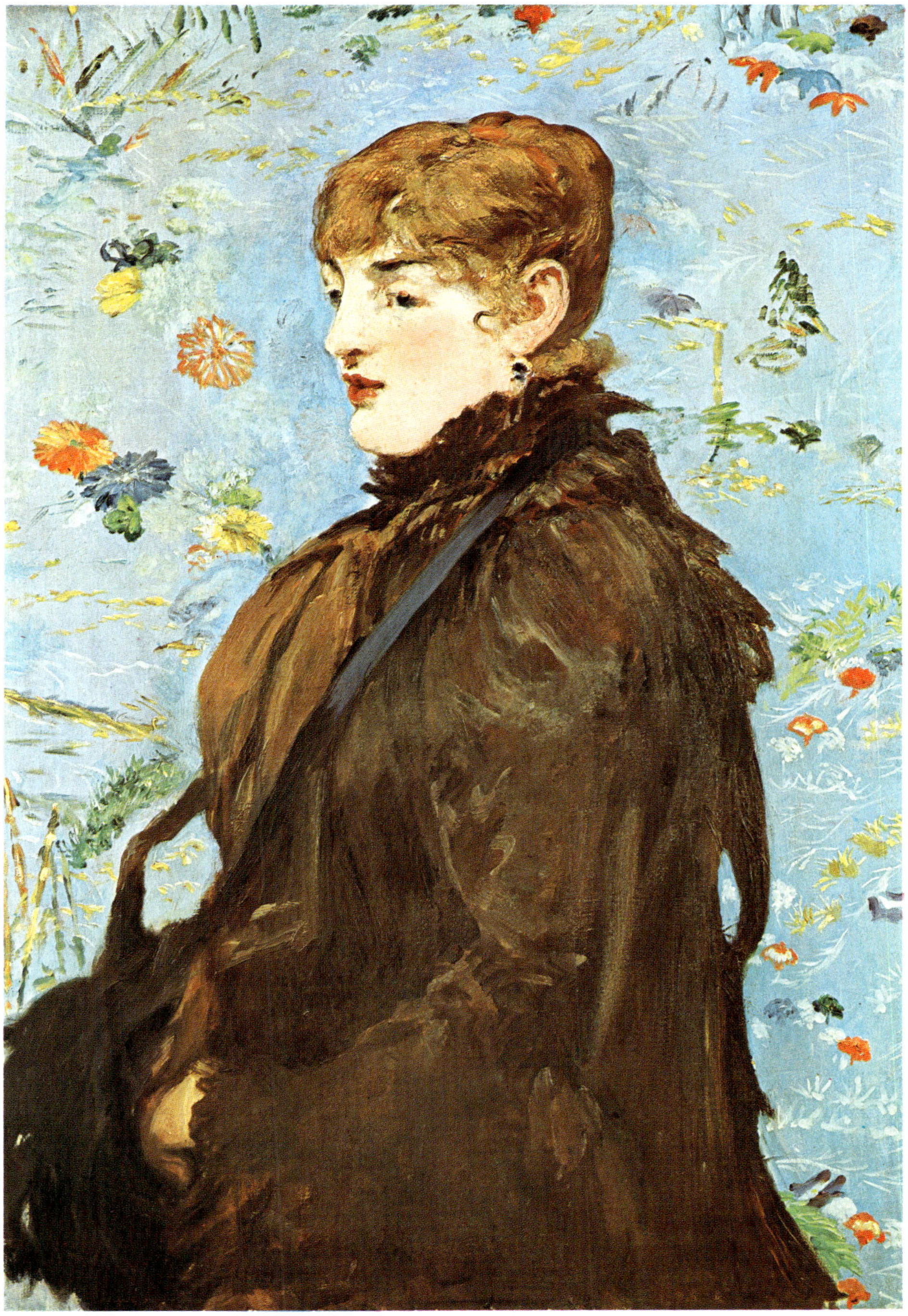

Editor in chief Anna Maria Mascheroni

Art director Luciano Raimondi

Text Sara Nathan

Translation Kerry Milis

Production Art, Bologna

Photo Credits Gruppo Editoriale Fabbri S.p.A., Milan

ISBN 2-89393-043-3

Printed in Italy by Gruppo Editoriale Fabbri S.p.A., Milan